A COMPASSIONATE GUIDE FOR A CO

THE DEEPLY HIDDEN ENEMY OF Y

"NO CONDEMNATION" + REJOICE IN YOUR GOD-GIVEN WORTH

FROM SHAME TO
GLORY
YOUR PATHWAY TO FREEDOM

KATHRYN W. CHAMBERLIN

Exulon
ELITE

This book is dedicated
to my husband, Ashby,
whose unwavering belief
in God's calling on my life
frequently lifted my challenged spirit with
"If it were easy, everybody would do it".

About the Book

"From Shame To Glory goes beyond aptly describing our universal struggle with debilitating shame. Kathryn Chamberlin nails the root in her chapter on idolatry, then gives us a step-by-step biblical pathway toward healing and freedom. This book would make a great small group study or Adult education curriculum."

Leslie Vernick, licensed counselor, coach, speaker, and author of the best selling books, *How to Act Right When Your Spouse Acts Wrong, The Emotionally Destructive Relationship*, and her newest book, *The Emotionally Destructive Marriage*.

leslie@leslievernick.com

Enriching the Relationships that Matter Most!

"Kathryn Chamberlin perfectly explicates the causes of and the relief from shame. *"From Shame to glory* is a magnificent read. As a clinical psychologist specializing in addictions and recovery, I can professionally and personally attest that dealing effectively with shame is key to success."

Richard H. Mikesell, Ph.D., senior editor of American Psychological Association's major volume in family therapy: *Integrating Family therapy: Handbook of Family Psychology and Systems Theory.*

"Since the early pages of the story of God, shame has been the central theme, and yet I will do just about anything to avoid it. I can't avoid the experience of shame, of course. None of us can. I'm a human, after all. I am finite but determined to be infinite, foolish but determined to craft my own wisdom, dependent but fiercely wanting to do it on my own. Thankfully it does not work.

If you have known the experience of wanting to crawl under a rock or to simply disappear or if you know what it's like to be flooded with rage toward yourself or others and you have no idea why-this book is for you. Kathryn will take your hand and slowly guide you through a courageous journey in exploring the sources and impact of shame in your life. It is not an easy journey, nor a quick one. But if you will take the time, you will find that your eyes are brighter, your countenance will be restored, and you can laugh at your own humanity. In other words, you'll taste the Kingdom and love of God."

> **Jan Proett**, author of *The Allure of Hope, Listening to Love*, and *Beauty and the Bitch: Grace for the Worst in Me*.

"God meets us in our guilt and shame to convict us of sin and bring us to salvation, forgiveness and healing through Jesus Christ. Guilt and shame are also tools of our adversary, who uses them to remind us of things God has forgiven and forgotten. Kathryn Chamberlin writes of the power of God over the power of Satan and reminds us of a love that, as the old hymn says, is 'deeper far than all my guilt and shame' because of the grace of God."

> **Cal Thomas**
> Syndicated and USA Today Columnist/Fox News Contributor

"This in-depth understanding of Shame from both clinical and biblical perspectives, is a must read for mental health professionals and their clients alike. Kathryn's book is chock full of information, insight and application for anyone on their journey From Shame to Glory."

> **Dawn Zimmerman, LPC**
> Director, McLean Bible Church Counseling Center

"I am most pleased to recommend this book to anyone interested in understanding the ins and outs of this most devastating condition known as SHAME. In From Shame to Glory, my long-time friend and colleague takes scholarly research into attachment theory, trauma recovery, codependency and neuroscience; blends it into a deep understanding of Christian teaching about God's character and His grace; and presents it through the eyes of a compassionate and skilled therapist. It is my hope that the reader will both gain understanding and experience a desire to help others in – or to engage him/herself in – the process of recovery which is outlined so clearly in the tested and proven path outlined in this book. May it encourage many along that path and may many come to experience that GLORY."

Kenneth O. Williams, MA, LCPC
Co-Founder and Executive Director,
Christian Counseling Associates, Inc.
Former international board president, Christian Association
for Psychological Studies

"A thorough study of different types of shame by a therapist who understands your pain, takes you to scripture, and leads you to hope."

Susan Alexander Yates
Bestselling author and speaker; author of *And Then I Had Kids,*
31 Days of Prayer for My Teen, How to Like the Ones You Love,
and others; married to John Yates, senior pastor The Falls Church

"Those fortunate to take this journey, *From Shame to Glory*, will gain rare insight into the ways shaming paralyzes the spirit and distorts personality. The reader will learn how surviving shame instinctively leads to habits of denial, perfectionism, emotional withdrawal or contempt for others. Kathryn Chamberlin offers a pathway to freedom from soul and relationship atrophy, great hope for inner healing and mutually safe, nurturing relationships."

Beverly Hubble Tauke, LCSW, Author of *Healing Your Family Tree* and contributing author, *Tending the Soul* and *Daily Seeds*

Acknowledgements

It is with delight that I take this opportunity to express my gratitude for the help, kindness, and encouragement that has been extended to me regarding this book.

First I want to describe two ministries at Halpine Baptist Church in Rockville, MD that gave me invaluable training in the application of God's word as applied to heartbreak and growth in a believer's life. In the adult education department, I was certified in Biblical Counseling where I found the "ah-ha" of my destiny. From the rewarding experience of lay counseling, I was inspired to attend graduate school for a master of social work degree. The other ministry, Ephesians Life Ministries, was serving families of alcoholics and offered me two group experiences required in my graduate program. After graduating I began a private practice and was blessed with many referrals from Ephesians Life Ministries. The co-founders, Rev. Jim Isom and Dr. Dee Bissell, and those who were blessed by their ministry share greatly in the wonderful 25 years of my privilege to serve the Lord as a psychotherapist.

Additionally, the invitations from Ephesians Life Ministries to speak on various topics to their groups, at their retreats, and their fund-raising seminars provided the opportunity to develop and present this material in myriad settings. Ultimately, the seminar attendees would be the impetus for converting the material into this book.

As a member of Fourth Presbyterian Church, Bethesda, MD, I am honored to teach various classes and present the shame seminar. The senior pastor, Dr. Robert Norris, afforded me much theological council and made me the awesome offer of writing the introduction for this book.

Early on in my struggle to go from presentation mode to book mode, my cousin, Becky Nelson, began to edit chapter by chapter. Later another cousin, Judy Henneberger, brought her expertise as a published professional musician to the editing role. Both of them take the relationship of cousin to a whole new level for me. Thank you, my dear cousins!

The first recommendation I have for a would-be author is to gather a prayer team. Marilyn Floyd is one of those friends whereby we muse that we have been through "everything" together. Marilyn, my cousin Judy, and my faithful-to-pray husband was my on-call prayer team. They provided the most essential support as I alerted them regularly to the specific issue or chapter that was on the screen of my computer. Please accept my thanks, Marilyn, Judy, and Ashby!

My large family has consistently believed that this book would happen and be a blessing. Especially, my husband who masterfully carved a fine line between encouraging and pushing. Our son, Todd, responded to my weary times with a challenge to set goals. Later he urged me toward the subtitle that I chose. Our daughter, Mary Ellen, a psychotherapist who is also writing a book, joined me to create what we affectionately call the "writecation." Our getaways to work on our books were personally heart-warming and productive times for this project. Others in the family would check in to note progress and encourage me to press on.

I am also very aware of my gratitude for those who attended the seminars over the years. Thank you to the churches and groups who hosted my presentations of this material. The material has evolved in large part because I continued to learn from researching shame and updated the material for the seminars. Likewise the urging of the attendees to transform the material into a book was courage-producing enough for me to undertake this work. You know who you are. Please know that your prompting was the catalyst for this endeavor.

Another group, though they are quite obvious, is friends and colleagues whose endorsements are here for you to read. Each one honored me with gifts of time, energy, and a willingness to publicly express their approval of and belief in the material. Please know that I am humbled by and appreciative of these gifts from each of you.

The tables in the varied chapters bear the professional touch of Natasha Gilliam, graphics designer (www.designenrg.com), whose excitement about the material was palpable. Other professionals at Xulon Press patiently fielded my questions with marked kindness.

Finally, I want to acknowledge my father and mother, Bill and Lottie Wood. I was never shamed as I came home each Sunday from church and preached a sermon. Atop my mother's sewing machine sat the sewing box my dad had made for her. That was just the right height to serve as my podium. From there I delivered scripture and commentary from a devotional called *The Upper Room*. To God be the glory for their faith-filled lives that blessed my life more than words can express.

Table of Contents

Introduction

The power of guilt and the shame that flows from it are indicators of the reality of evil in our world. Such evil has emotional, physical, and spiritual dimensions. The power of shame is always toxic and has the power to consume the whole person, frequently robbing the individual of peace, joy, and real pleasure. The one affected by shame all too often suffers under the sense of being permanently damaged and so understands himself as being inferior. This sense of being defective leads to behaviors that range from the violent and destructive to complete withdrawal under a sense of worthlessness.

In this book, a gifted therapist and committed Christian brings the biblical perspective on these realities into a focus that avoids the condemnatory legalism that is the all too frequent response of Christians. Instead there is an examination and encouragement to find the power of grace in the life of the Christian. What is combined is an accurate theological truth applied in a way that is practical with a power that is healing. Emotions, will, and actions are all examined and united in a way that can bring freedom and restoration to the individual. Here is made clear that the good news of the gospel means that shame can be healed. With the skill of a physician of the emotions, the author offers a road map for the believer to return to well-being and the peace that comes from knowing we are accepted by the grace of One whose acceptance of us matters most.

Much more than a "self help" book this is a careful explanation of the gospel method of applying the grace of God and the triumph of the cross to lives that have been disfigured and thought patterns that have been made dysfunctional by the reality of sin. It is a work that brings hope to many who have lived under despair.

As a pastor I can attest to the value of this study as I have witnessed its power in the lives of many who have experienced the wounds inflicted by living under the power of guilt and the shame it brings. At first hand I have witnessed the ministry of the author and the power of that ministry over many years to bring health and hope to those afflicted by these curses and suffering from the condemnation of those who would seek to impose an unbiblical legalism on them. Here is a proven way forward into the healing power of the grace of Christ.

Dr. Robert M. Norris, Senior Pastor
Fourth Presbyterian Church
5500 River Road
Bethesda, MD 20816

Preface

As a young bride, I wanted to put my best foot forward with my new husband's family. One evening I was making the best of a visit with his contentious uncle, when suddenly time stood still. The old man's piercing eyes glared at me from a critical, scowling face. I shriveled moment by moment.

He snarled, "You're a nurse, aren't you?"

I froze. Proud of my profession, his belittling snarl made me regret my nursing degree at that moment–a haunting moment suspended in time. Paralysis had captured my body. Panic surfaced as desperation–desperate to find the proverbial hole in the wall and disappear to escape his scathing scowl.

Without waiting for more of an answer than a nod from a frozen stiff body, he railed on. A question exploded from somewhere deep in his contemptuous soul. "What are the layers of the skin?!?", he demanded. The answer remained locked up somewhere in my, by now, non-functioning brain along with my name, and other such minor, irretrievable details. A barely audible whisper betrayed my desperate heart: "I don't know." This discovery seemed to satisfy every pompous bone in his body. He bellowed: "... damn kids don't know anything now a days."

I managed to hold myself together, keeping this secret: that under his venomous attack–everything of value had been drained from my being. The young bride, full of hope, joy and confidence, felt punctured and powerless. As soon as it was socially acceptable, I headed home, a filleted self – feeling lifeless with no guts and no backbone.

Years later after training as a therapist and entering into the privilege of helping people with emotional pain, I noticed that pain like I experienced that day with my husband's uncle often originates and is perpetuated in relationships. I also discovered a common denominator. Regardless of the problem that motivated men and women to seek counsel, when we probed for understanding of the angst, the confusion, the sense of defeat, we inevitably encountered an experience named shame.

It started becoming clear to me and the courageous clients in my office that shame was at work in their frustrations, their disappointments, and unsatisfying relationships. Anger began stirring in my soul about this experience called shame, this experience that was driving their pain.

We also began to understand the role of shame in their pursuit of interests or their avoidance of pursuing their interests. It was as if budding passions and dreams from long ago were imprisoned in their mental attics, bound by cobwebs of shame. What had exiled those hopes and interests, now long deposed and forgotten? Furthermore what had troubled individuals, their families, and their communities been deprived of because of stultifying shame? As we courageously and cautiously made our way into the attic, we began to understand shame as an enemy – an enemy of God's beloved and the creativity He designed in those He loves. The enemy was pervasive and destructive beyond description. Now that I had discovered this stealthiest enemy of the soul, I had to do something.

I declared war on this enemy by adding research to my clinical experience. I discovered shame described as the most painful emotion that humans can suffer, the universality of shame (no one reaches adulthood without accumulating some degree of shame) and its inhibitory effect that restricts our explorations and developments of that which is within us.

Discovering, dismantling, and defeating the torturous, imprisoning enemy and helping to restore lives toward vibrant, life-giving wholeness in their God-given worth became the focus of my life's work. The following chapters are dedicated to helping us together to defeat this life-depleting assailant called shame.

In both the private world of my office and in my seminars, I witnessed an undeniable transformation in those impacted by the material gathered from my research and clinical experience. Responses have been revelations such as, "I never recognized that I have a problem with perfectionism!" "Now I am responding differently to guilt than I am to shame." "I am learning to turn to God, instead of hiding from him." "Everybody needs to hear this."

May this book continue to expose this enemy and be to its readers a profound tipping point into a deeper intimacy with God and with their loved ones. May it also be the release needed by countless children of God to risk the pursuit of their talents and dreams. This is my prayer and my motivation for writing this book.

Please score the following "Shame Test"[1] by checking the 10 items with one of the 7 options. After totaling your score, look to the guidelines for interpreting your score. Even this brief list of how shame may manifest in your life may be helpful for getting acquainted with shame.

Shame Test

Read the following statements: then, choose the term from the top of the test which best describes your response. Put the number above that term in the blank beside each statement.

1	2	3	4	5	6	7
Always	Very Often	Often	Sometimes	Seldom	Very Seldom	Never

_____ 1. I often think about past failures or experiences of rejection.

_____ 2. There are certain things about my past which I cannot recall without experiencing strong, painful emotions (i.e. guilt, shame, anger, fear, etc.).

_____ 3. I seem to make the same mistakes over and over again.

_____ 4. There are certain aspects of my character that I want to change, but I don't believe I can ever successfully do so.

_____ 5. I feel inferior.

_____ 6. There are aspects of my appearance that I cannot accept.

_____ 7. I am generally disgusted with myself.

_____ 8. I feel that certain experiences have basically ruined my life.

_____ 9. I perceive of myself as an immoral person.

_____ 10. I feel that I have lost the opportunity to experience a complete and wonderful life.

_____ Total (Add up the numbers you have placed in the blanks.)

Interpretation of score for: The Shame Test

57 – 70

God has apparently given you a very strong appreciation for His love and unconditional acceptance. You seem to be free of the shame that plagues most people. (Some people who score this high are either greatly deceived, or have become callous to their emotions as a way to suppress pain.)

47 – 56

Shame controls your responses rarely, or only in certain situations. Again, the only major exceptions are those who are not honest with themselves.

36 – 46

When you experience emotional problems, they may relate to a sense of shame. Upon reflection, you will probably relate many of your previous decisions to a poor sense of self-worth. Many of your future decisions will also be affected by lost self-esteem unless you take direct action to overcome it.

27 – 36

Shame forms a generally negative backdrop to your life. There are probably few days that you are not in some way affected by shame. Unfortunately, this robs you of the joy and peace your salvation is meant to bring.

0 -26

Experiences of shame dominate your memory and have probably resulted in a great deal of depression. These problems will remain until some definitive action is taken. This condition will not simply disappear; time alone cannot heal your pain. You need to experience deep healing in your self-concept, in your relationship with God, and in your relationships with others. You must deal with its root issue.

Chapter 1

Shame Attack

It is equally dangerous to man to know God
without knowing his own wretchedness, and
to know his own wretchedness without knowing God.[1]

Pensees, Blaise Pascal

While driving to The Falls Church Christmas concert on a Friday night, I noticed one tiny house displaying two huge, puffy, inflated lawn ornaments amidst the twinkly lights –a giant snowman and a Santa as tall as the house. On Sunday morning, 36 hours later, I drove past the same house on my way to church. The snowman and the Santa, rather than towering over the house, lay flat, completely smooshed on the lawn. All the puff had de-poofed. Had I not seen them earlier, I would not have recognized them. They were now huge flat plastic pancakes devoid of identity. They lay severed from the air generator that had kept them inflated. Santa and the snowman lay completely kaput.

They had lost their core connection.

My friend sent me this parable of the puffy lawn ornaments as a metaphor for the experience of shame that you are about to encounter in this book.

Shame! You are to be commended for picking up this book, opening it, and beginning to read it. Shame! The distasteful word makes us want to push it away and take a step back from it. It is a stomach turner. You may want to move on to read something more uplifting. Surely no good thing can emanate from a book about shame?!?

And yet the title of the book already reveals to the brave reader that something good this way comes. So, all brave souls, journey with me into this secretive, off-putting, stomach-turning experience of shame. Descend with me into descriptions of the experience and the origins of the accumulated shame within us. Persevere as you encounter the role that shame plays in perfectionism, integrity, creativity, guilt, and inferiority. Be willing to name the shame-laden experiences as they rise from the pain of your past. Be open to recognizing your own shaming behaviors to which you have resorted for helping you to cope with life. Stay the course. Feel hope arise within you as the light begins to dawn on this dark, destructive condition called shame. Stay the course until the healing power of Jesus Christ becomes evident – until the turning of shame into glory begins to be a reality for you.

The condition of shame may be pervasive in our souls – so constant and influential in our psyche that it is a chronic condition. When shame is constantly influencing our choices and behaviors, the personality is described as shame-based or shame-prone. However, the focus of this book is not on the chronic condition known as shame-based. Our focus is on the acute, specific time when shame floods our being. This time has a sudden onset with very definitive responses in our bodies, in our mental capacities, and in our emotions. The name for this sudden, overwhelming, acute takeover of our being is a shame attack. Those who suffer the more chronic experience of shame also suffer the being suddenly flooded by shame experience. And so the understanding and the healing of shame is the same, regardless of chronicity or acuteness.

First we must get familiar with this experience called a shame attack. The lists below come from several people's descriptions of feelings when shame suddenly attacks. The lists seem long, because everyone does not relate to the same descriptive phrases. By the time you finish reading the lists, it is hoped that you will understand the experience of a shame attack—that you will have the ah-ha of "been there, done that." Please note that while shame attacks hit suddenly, their ending is more like a fading away.

Descriptions of feelings during a shame attack:

- A tormenting sense of inferiority and sinfulness
- A loss of face
- A state of disgrace
- Social inadequacy
- A feeling of worthlessness

Thoughts about self during a shame attack:

- I should be damned.
- I have no personal integrity.
- I am devoid of goodness.
- I am full of sin.
- I am utterly reprehensible
- I am hopeless and helpless in my defectiveness. (There is no way to relieve the matter, no way to restore the balance of things.)
- I have failed as a human being…there is nothing I can do to make up for it.
- I am completely diminished or insufficient as a person.
- I am worthy of rejection.
- I am not fully valid as a human being.

To put the above lists into a nutshell, we suffer a loss of worth. To varying degrees, our sense of worth and value has painfully been diminished or disappeared altogether. Since the definition of a shame attack revolves around diminishment of the self or loss of worth, we will consider the shame attack as an unhealthy experience. An all-important theme of this book is this: any loss of worth is completely unnecessary and, by Biblical standards, is also particularly and especially inappropriate! This truth is a bedrock belief of the healing process. Therefore the operative definition of shame, loss of worth, excludes any concept of healthy shame.

Some argue that shame serves a virtuous purpose, that it can motivate us to do the right thing.[2] Later we will see why shame is not needed to deter us from ungodly behavior. We'll also see that shame has been taken care of and dealt with divinely. In our freedom from shame, we are not to participate in it in any manner! (This concept of all shame being unhealthy saves us from analytical sorting, i.e. am I experiencing unhealthy shame or healthy shame.) Therefore all experiences of shame create an opportunity for cleansing and healing. Despite all shame being unhealthy, we will learn how all feelings of shame create an invitation to draw nearer to our Lord. Experiences of shame offer an opportunity for growth and sanctification. We will experience a shame attack as an entreaty to discover how God means this pain for good. A shame attack can remind us that healing awaits us as does deeper trust in and closer relationship with God. We can know the transformation of our shame to His glory.

As one expert on the subject of shame states, (previously noted), "One has simply failed as a human being...and... there is nothing I can do to make up for it".[3] After studying the above lists, I was able to determine that I had known this experience called a shame attack many times. My own description (shared in The Preface) would be added to the list of thoughts about self during a shame attack: I experience myself like a filleted fish... no guts... no backbone. I encourage you to choose a description from those listed with which you resonate and/or add your own.

Shame has the distinction of being called the most painful emotion known to mankind. Hopefully all readers are now able to identify the painful experience of having a shame attack. Being able to recognize the experience of a shame attack will make the remainder of the book an untold blessing of a pathway to healing.

Let us continue beyond the emotional pain of suddenly seeming worthless to the physiological and mental dimension of a shame attack. Here's what's going on in our body. Immediately one may think of blushing, of embarrassment. But besides blushing, there is a component of confusion. One description of the confusion reads like this: "Persons in this condition lose their presence of mind, and utter singularly inappropriate remarks. They are often much distressed, stammer, and make awkward movements or strange grimaces."[4] Can you hear the confusion in the quote, the inability to think and speak as we usually do? Has anybody ever not been there?

In several places in the Bible, we see shame and confusion in the same sentence of a plea for God's help.

> *"Let them be put to shame and confusion who seek my life!" Psalm 70:2 (The Revised Standard Version)*

You may recall some of the battles from the Bible and how important the element of confusion was in victory for God's chosen people.

When experiencing shame, we display body language which indicates that our sense of self has been exposed as defective. We become desperate to disappear. The face and the eyes (our window of the soul) particularly reveal this discomfort. We avoid eye contact by averting the eyes, possibly staring at the floor, with eyes and head down. Or there may be defensive body language attempting to ward off feeling shame by the frozen stare into an offenders' eyes, the head back, and a look of contempt. So this experience of a shame attack involves our whole being – our body, our thinking, feelings and actions. It really has the power to derail us–as our entire being gets caught up in a shame attack.

You know these moments, we all have them. All is well with us. We are okay. Then something is said, done, or perceived. Suddenly enormous panic floods our internal world. We have absolutely no control over the instantaneous confusion and embarrassment that is taking over our being. Our system goes into overload. We are into the experience in a nano second with no ability to stop it. If we could freeze the moment into slow motion and discover what is happening, we would most often find the power of shame driving the experience.

Shame carries the distinction of being the best-hidden, most insidious experience in the make-up of human beings. The stored shame is usually so well hidden that it offers no clue that it is lurking in that secret place. It is exiled out of our awareness. Therefore, we have no suspicions that shame may be the root cause of regrettable behaviors. Shame becomes our soul's enemy working behind the scenes, in secret, to produce, "…without parallel a sickness of the soul."[5] Shame does not always operate by itself. It can be a tool or a means to an end that is used by the greatest enemy of our soul, Satan, for our destruction. The Evil One's sole objective is to destroy the glory/beauty which God intends to grow in us. And one of the best tools he can use is the inhibiting and destructive force called shame.

This incredibly painful experience naturally motivates us to avoid it at all costs. If a shame attack has the power to wipe us out as human beings, why not avoid it at all costs? What's wrong with this game plan? Because the attack is only a symptom of the sickness. Shame entered into the picture and into the depths of our souls at The Fall. It has been present and profoundly influential since that time. Then many of our life's experiences added to that storehouse of shame. To grapple with shame's devastation in our lives creates the possibility of healing and freedom that some of us cannot even imagine yet. The curious phenomenon of shame is that avoiding it can drive us into hiding our real self, resulting in lost potential and self-defeating behaviors forever. Or it can usher us to the foot of the cross where our pervasive need for a Savior is met in untold goodness. The good news is that the choice is ours. Scripture extends the invitation:

> *"See, I lay a stone in Zion, a chosen and precious*
> *cornerstone, and the one who trusts in Him will never*

be put to shame." 1Peter2:6 (The Revised Standard
Version)

Trusting in the goodness and vision of glory that God has for his children is little more than a pipedream for many of us. Caught up in our determination to avoid the devastating pain of a shame attack, we must defend our souls against experiencing a shame attack. We choose hiding over healing. And in this choice, we forego the incredible adventure into deeper intimacy with God.

During a shame attack the only choices seem to be the classic defense mechanisms of fight, flight, or freeze – not redemption of lost potential, not the transformation of shame to glory. The option instead of self-defense is an exploration into the interior, into the inner man. The option is to invite God to search our hearts. The journey into the heart in search of shame and its effects is not an easy one. But the promise of forgiveness, healing, transformation, and redemption beckons. And our willingness for God to journey into our hidden storehouse is essential if we heed our call to mature in Christ, to experience our shame transformed to His glory.

Now really the core of what's going on in a shame attack is that the self is feeling exposed. It is as if we are "impaled under a magnifying glass".[6] And guess what is being exposed or magnified? Could it be our wonderful, nice, competent, adequate selves? In our dreams!

We are feeling less worthy than any other human being because something we consider defective, something we experience as unacceptable, something that we did not want anybody to know, something we did not want exposed has just been exposed. And the authoritative finality of "...shame, shame, shame" rushes in as the worst possible verdict due to shame's distinction as the most painful emotion known to mankind. And now the judge delivers the verdict with each whack of his gavel, "...shame, shame, shame.... Case closed."

An old TV program from quite a bit of yesteryears, featured a character known as a judge. His arrival on the set would always be announced, "Here come de judge!" Now we assume that the judgment of "shame" has been delivered from this official elected to rule over mankind with required standards for making it as a human being on planet earth. Well, "Here come de judge." But guess what? "De judge" is within. We have a resident judge. And he doesn't miss an opportunity to rain down the verdict, to deliver the worst of news – "shame, shame, shame".

Perhaps hopelessness wells up within you as you recognize your resident judge. You may be familiar with the tendency to beat up on yourself. It may seem like a permanent default mechanism lodged deep in an unreachable place. So we may begin to wonder about healing? Is God's transforming power relegated to the pipedream? Let us look to Scripture for encouragement. Verses abound about God's desire for our growth. Hear His prophetic word:

> *"Instead of their shame my people will receive a double portion, and instead of disgrace they will*

rejoice in their inheritance; and so they will inherit a double portion in their land, and everlasting joy will be theirs." Isaiah 61:7

Or be reminded of His goodness by Saint Paul:

"Everyone who trusts in Him will never be put to shame" Romans 10:11

Since we are usually doing a good job of avoiding a shame attack, our discovery of the well-hidden shame usually begins with the less hidden parts of our life. Sometimes we start with failed relationships, lost dreams, or that haunting sense of underachieving. Or sometimes we start by seeing habits and behaviors that are annoying to others or self defeating. For example look at this very short list that will most likely ring familiar to you:

Have you ever noticed someone who:

... gets furious when his son gets a low mark on his report card
... refuses to consider suggestions to write a book
... gets a headache cleaning the house when expecting guests
... consistently rejects a compliment
... responds to almost all situations with humor
... habitually demeans self
... stays involved with pornography despite vows to abstain
... cringes at the thought of asking for a favor
... is very invested in never being wrong
... scolds a child for tears or anger or fears
... copes with rejection or disappointment by eating

The only realistic ending for this list is etc., etc., etc. The habits or personality traits that may be driven by shame are limitless. This unlimited list of frustrating and destructive traits are signs that shame, in its deathly secrecy, is working against God's desire for us to be His glory.

And then there is another dimension to this list of patterns. And this is the dimension that frequently is extolled as Christian virtues. So this group of traits may be surprising or some may argue that these are Godly behaviors:

> ... gives constantly to others but doesn't receive
> ... gives until they are angry, exhausted, and emptied of everything
> ... is consumed with others' needs, no thought of their own
> ... is driven by the good deeds they should do
> ...settles for nothing less than perfect
> ... maintains image of always being on top of their game
> ... is determined to be nice by never differing/always approving
> ... focuses on pleasing everyone at any cost

This, too, is an open-ended list. The behaviors that made the list, and those that did not, cover such a wide range, that the list is best ended with *ad infinitum*. Behaviors, attitudes, and beliefs that are rooted in shame are limitless. Some would claim that certain of these behaviors are good things, defending the behavior with, "I do this because I am a nice person". Others may bemoan some of them saying "I wish I would not do that". Yet others may see these habits as severe problems and be crying out for help, "This is miserable, and I cannot stop it."

The people who experience these seemingly unrelated patterns and countless others, may share something quite significant–the same root of shame. The origin and the perpetuator of these varied patterns may be the same – shame. The root problem of shame is usually hidden and offers no clue that it is causing certain behaviors. Thus you, too, like me, may be surprised by shame.

Why is it that shame, this sickness, is so typically hidden from our own awareness? This painful, sometimes devastating, nature of a shaming experience causes us to determine to forget that it ever happened. Even as children when we experienced shame, we attempted to bury this awful feeling; bury it away from our awareness and out of our memories. And, since those early burial days, we have worked hard to avoid any reminders of that experience. Therefore, we have very little indication that it is there – much less that it is causing behavior patterns that we would like to change. The expression that feelings may be buried but are buried alive, is never truer than when the feeling is shame.

And so it's time to issue a warning. And the final warning centers around the potential pain. Not only is it an incredibly painful emotion, it is contagious. You may notice that reading another's shaming experience can bring on some feeling of shame for you. Possibly what you have read so far stirs some shame within you. As I researched and created this material, I noticed at times I needed to take a break. I was experiencing this unpleasant, undesirable feeling simply by studying it.

I want to encourage you to muster up your courage and press into the material. If you have a friend who would be willing to read and share with you – great! Someone to share in what you are learning and feeling as you press on would be an untold blessing. Pray for such a friend who would explore the dynamic of shame with you.

Part one of the book attempts to expose the existence of this hidden and hazardous material buried deep in our souls. We begin with the assumption that shame is a part of everyone's experience, that none of us have escaped the effects of being born a finite creation, living in a broken, sinful world. None of us have been raised in perfect, unflawed families. Such a family does not exist. This book is an offering of hope not only to those severely shame-based but also to those of us who function well, safely avoiding shame attacks, unaware of underground shame that governs much of what we do or do not do. We are many – the man or woman next door, our siblings, our friends, our spouses, our colleagues, and ourselves who admit frustrations with relationships and jobs. We might have a vague awareness of untapped, God-given potential. But we mostly live into the next day and then the next without major disruption or major joy. Generally, we have managed our lives to work satisfactorily and only occasionally feel a little malaise from playing it safe.

We become resigned to our negative behaviors. These behaviors range from entrenched habits or addictions to an occasional compelling "out of character" behavior which we may think of as having "reared its ugly head". It goes unnoticed that avoiding shame drives many of these negative behaviors as well as those that are deemed positive, but actually are negative. For example, taking undue responsibility for another's happiness may be seen as virtuous and loving while it truly is not Spirit-led behavior. Our shame-avoiding ways are an exquisite management plan of control that leaves little space for God to work in us according to His purpose.

"For it is God who works in you to will and to act according to His good purpose." Philippians 2:13

The following chapters of this book begins our exploration into dynamics that include the relationship of shame to creativity, anger, contempt towards self and others, relationship failure, attraction to perfectionism, and even the use of humor. We will examine relationship-damaging behaviors that are defensive–behaviors that are designed to avoid shame. It is here that we will see the passing of shame from one generation to the next. We will see choices that we have made that maintain the safety of our own souls, specifically, safety from the risk of a shame attack. We will then be in a position to choose to trust God as the keeper of our souls in His desire that we mature–deepening our intimacy, passion, and capacity to love and be loved.

This side of heaven, we will continue to encounter shame. The question changes from, "How will I avoid shame?" to "How will I respond to shame?" The surprising truth is that a Godly response to a shame attack brings with it the potential to draw closer to Him. Paradoxically, this foe, this enemy of our soul, provides a gateway to intimacy with God. In the arena of shame is found the truth that what Satan intended for evil, God used for good.

> *"You intended to harm me, but God intended it for good to accomplish what is now being done. "Genesis 50:20 (The Revised Standard Version)*

Our prayer is that we develop a respect, knowledge and appreciation of shame's harm and shame's potential gift and to choose to walk through that gateway.

Finally we'll look at what to do with this "gift" we have discovered. We will examine some guidelines for seeking healing. The guidelines describe an intentional posture for healing. They are not the, "Ten Steps to Rid Your Life of Shame". Our healing is ultimately dependent on the power of God. Though God is our healer, He asks for our participation. He asks us to choose:

> *"This day I call heaven and earth as witnesses against you that I have set before you life and death, blessings and curses. Now choose life, so that you and your children may live and that you may love the Lord your God, listen to his voice and hold fast to him." Deuteronomy 30: 19-20a*

This choice of life includes pain. Often God heals our wounds by walking us right into the hurt again. He clearly reveals in His word that He yearns to begin the process of healing shame.

"O ye sons of men, how long will you turn my glory into shame..."Psalm 4:2 (The King James Version)

Although the transformation of our shame to His glory won't be completed in this life, the process itself will strengthen our faith. In addition to a strengthened faith, the healing of our shame will diminish our fear of being who we were designed to be. Surely in proportion to the healing, we will be increasingly able to love well–to be His hands, feet, and heart as we labor in our great commission. Is it any wonder that God longs to enter into the healing process with us?

Healing means that shame is transformed into glory. Glory is not a word we use comfortably. Many of us have had an automatic resistance to believing anything about us is glorifying of God. Despite scripture's insistence that we are to glorify God, we live as if that is mission impossible. Or at best, our ability to abide by the rules and live mistake-free is our attempt to glorify Him. This book challenges us to shift our focus from avoiding a shame attack neither by keeping the rules and avoiding mistakes nor by avoiding the pain via addictions. Will we shift our focus toward the healing of shame by choosing to journey into territory toxic with shame-laden land mines? We will learn to hope in the presence of God as we risk entering that toxic territory. Though shame is a hellish emotion, we can remember the psalmist declaring,

> *"If I go up to the heavens, you are there; if I make my bed in the depths, you are there." Psalm 139:8*

He has extended an invitation for healing and intimacy with Him. It is the ravages of shame that lead us to decline the invitation and thus we miss out relationally, as well as missing the mark of our creative potential. He asks us to bear His glory. We have a choice in what we will bear. We must choose between shame and glory. Will you journey with me into that choice?

Chapter 2

Innate Shame

"We have invented an unnecessary obligation to be as God."[1]

Margaret Alter

Those of us who have had the privilege and the challenge of spending much time with the "no-me-do-it" toddler set will be very familiar with the following scenario by the above quoted author. This is shame in action:

"The small girl ahead of me in the grocery line that Passover season must have been about two-and-a-half years old. She pleaded with her mother to give her the largest box of matzos to carry. As a good parent, the mother squatted down at eye level to talk quietly with her child. She explained that the box, almost the size of the child, was too heavy for the little girl to lift. The mother offered the child a smaller box in substitution. The girl wailed in protest. At last, the mother took the box out of the grocery cart and gave it to the child.

And, of course, the box of matzos was too heavy for her, and it slid through her clasped arms to the floor. Immediately the child threw herself on the floor in despair, sobbing inconsolably. The mother then quietly placed the box in the cart, paid for her groceries, picked up her daughter, and left. When my groceries rolled into check-out, the checker said through her teeth, 'I'd like to get my hands on that kid'. I did not reply. I felt sorry for the mother. She had been a model of patience. My two children were in high school at the time, but I remembered the early years of potential public humiliation. But being a parent was only one reason for withholding judgment.

> I was fairly confident that I had within me my own shrieking two-year-old who threatened disintegration when confronted with life's limits. My internal "child" had her own matzo box she wanted to carry. She said things like: 'Chocolate chip cookies are *not* fattening!' The child had taken to herself a grandeur that she could not accomplish and the result was crushing humiliation. Certainly in this way the child represents all of us in our human longing to live grandly, graciously, easily beyond limits, admired, and applauded, 'fulfilling our potential', godlike in our essence."[2]

This chapter addresses the particular type of shame, innate shame, experienced by that little girl. How many times has each of us overreached to do the impossible? And how many of us, along with the writer quoted above, recognize that yearning within to be the exceptional achiever? According to the number of times in our toddlerhood that we insisted on unrealistic deeds, our little systems may have experienced this type of shame. Early on we began amassing this innate shame. This defiance of our human limitations is a refusal to accept God's design. To some degree many of us continue to battle our condition called finitude. We recognize an infinite God and, like Adam and Eve, we find ourselves striving to join Him. Finiteness is simply not good enough.

Parents walk such a fine line when a child is exhibiting this overreaching tendency. The child ventures into the risk of failure and shame. The parenting that supports children in trying new endeavors but protects them from too much failure and shame is truly an art form. The question is not even–have I had these shaming experiences whereby I was unrealistically overreaching, and failure brought me into shame? The question is: What toll have those experiences taken? How have these failures impacted the development of my personality? And, as if these are not enough questions, how am I continuing to declare that my finiteness is unacceptable? In what ways am I driven to disown my sinful nature and my human limitations? When am I demanding perfection in my performance? How often do I lose my sense of worth because my humanness shows up? The unrealistic demands are a whip some of us crack to intensify the striving, to defy our God-created finitude. This inherited tendency to want to be god-like can be quite subtle. Because of its prevalence and subtlety, we will examine our desire for perfection carefully in chapter 5.

So let us return to the de-poofed, deflated lawn ornaments discussed in chapter 1. How might their collapse metaphorically speak to Adam and Eve's plummet in paradise? And how does their infamous fall create the beginning of our consideration of shame?

We start with a focus on the story of God's magnificent creation of all things:

> *"For this reason a man will leave his father and mother and be united to his wife, and they will become one flesh. The man and his wife were both naked, and they felt no shame." Genesis 2: 24-25*

This my friends is paradise. Adam and Eve are given multiple, awesome blessings in this utopia. Certainly their relationship with each other and with God is their crowning glory of blessings. They have the potential to enjoy the challenge of subduing the earth. They have the potential for feeling accomplishment in managing the remainder of His creation. And most importantly, they enjoy a lifeline of His life-giving Spirit. This is virtually a connection to their Creator that infuses love, direction, worth, and value. Among these glorious blessings in paradise is nestled one limitation. This limitation restricts a type of knowledge and the power that accompanies that knowledge. This knowledge is designed only for the realm of the infinite. God's finite children are excluded from equality within the Holy Trinity. They are denied or spared the knowledge of good and evil. We can conclude that His children were to be spared this knowledge because we know His creation is good. And that creation includes the way He separated the infinite from the finite – the design for an incredibly close connection, but not a merger of The Trinity and His children.

We continue in The Garden of Eden. Now the plot thickens: In the midst of this abundant bounty and life-giving intimacy – awesome blessings – in slithers temptation. Evil arrives in paradise. If we could create sound effects, we would fill the background with dark, troubled bass tones drumming in the tempter. These bone-chilling tones so eerily signify the approach of evil with God's children targeted. The crosshairs mark the exact target–Adam and Eve's contentment with God's creation. Their contentment is in jeopardy. The evil one draws a bead on their contentment with their condition of finite. The temptation to abandon their contentment with being His finite children is in the making. God's command defined the one limitation that carried a deathly consequence:

> *"but you must not eat from the tree of the knowledge of good and evil, for when you eat of it you will surely die." Genesis 2: 17*

The temptation to become as God takes on full force. The lie is executed. God's character is assassinated:

"You will not surely die…For God knows that when you eat of it your eyes *will be opened , and you will be like God…" Genesis 3:4-5*

Adam and Eve abandoned their contentment in Paradise where they ruled in partnership – where they loved and were loved in communion with the Spirit of God- to reach for something more. *Matthew Henry's Commentary* describes the lure of the evil one:

"He aims to make [Adam and Eve] discontented with their present state, as if it were not so good as it might be, and should be. He tempts them to seek preferment, as if they were fit to be gods. Satan ruined himself by desiring to be like the Most High, therefore he sought to infect our first parents with the same desire, that he might ruin them too."[3]

This disobedience was a refusal to be finite. Adam and Eve were overreaching from their creation as limited creatures. They contemptuously turned on their finiteness screaming to the heavens, "not good enough, God!" "Thanks, but no thanks." "We want more control." "Your plan is insufficient!" "We refuse your design." You are fired!" "We got a better offer and we are taking it and it will be so worth it!"

This refusal to settle for being finite, this overreaching to be infinite, unleashed a torrent of consequences. A colloquial expression for that infamous rebellion might sound like this: A lot came down that day. And so this book explores one of the devastating consequences – SHAME. This dark, destructive experience called shame shows up immediately after the enactment of the rebellious uprising. Adam and Eve not only hide from each other, they hide from God. They hide from the God with whom they had walked in the garden everyday. They had known sweet fellowship, intimate communion in their close relationship with Him.

> *"...so they sewed fig leaves together and made coverings for themselves and they hid from the Lord God..." Genesis 3: 7-8*

So as a direct consequence of their rebellion that day, Adam and Eve severed themselves from the lifeline of His life-giving Spirit. Spiritually, they die. They are no longer connected to His infusing love and direction. They unplug the connection, losing His life-giving source of worth and identity. Like the puffy lawn ornaments they loose their power source. Adam and Eve are now totally different creatures. Disconnected, their identity becomes an enigma. With God's love no longer infusing them with worth, they succumb to shame. They had stood tall full of the worth and value continuously infused by their Creator. Being created in His image had filled them with a dignity that set them apart from all other objects of His creation. He was the creator and the sustainer of their worth and value. The loss is immeasurable. The fallout of The Fall is colossal damage. Adam and Eve overreached to get more worth and value and lost the worth and value they had. They lost their sense of being "very good". His children are devastated. And his children's children will be born with a desire to overreach, to reach beyond their finiteness. The succeeding generations right on down to you and me are born with a discontent about being finite. We are born with a sinful nature that causes us to strive to be like God. The discontent that causes us to strive is a part of our inheritance. How might this look in each of our lives? How does this innate shame that is woven into our being show up in our attitudes, in our behaviors, in our desires? Even in our prayers?

Even in our prayers. I am reminded in my own experience of this very thing. In the early years of my spiritual journey, I discovered people who had an intimate relationship with God, who experienced a deep friendship with Jesus. And they led study/prayer groups in which I was blessed to be a participant. And so as I became comfortable praying aloud, I clearly remember praying that God would make me worthy of all that He had done for me. That is right. Though I knew I did not deserve the blessings of His grace, I had yet to realize that I would never be worthy of His grace. If we use the classic description of grace as unmerited favor, then we know in an automatic way that we are not and never will be worthy of his grace. So we are born with a discontent that causes us to strive to be like God and experience shame when we fail. This kind of Catch 22 dilemma needs a solution. It needs nothing short of redemption.

Let's return to the scriptures and breathe a sigh of relief as the story of that redemption unfolds. Isaiah prophesied to God's chosen people:

"But Israel will be saved by the Lord with an everlasting salvation; you will never be put to shame or disgraced, to ages everlasting." Isaiah 45:17

"Do not be afraid; you will not suffer shame. Do not fear disgrace; you will not be humiliated. You will forget the shame of your youth..." Isaiah 54:4

"Your covenant with death will be annulled, and your agreement with hell will not stand..." Isaiah 28:18

"Instead of their shame my people will receive a double portion, and instead of disgrace they will rejoice in their inheritance; and so they will inherit a double portion in their land, and everlasting joy will be theirs." Isaiah 61:7

Remember this is an in inheritance that embodied the discontent and striving. Our finiteness is also a part of this inheritance. Is Isaiah really prophesying that we will rejoice in this inheritance? There is no mistaking that we will not merely accept our finiteness, we will rejoice in it. We are going to rejoice in our inheritance. How can it be? How would we ever rejoice in that with which we were so discontent that we disobeyed God in order to move out of it? We rebelled against God in order to move from being finite to become infinite.

Again we return to the prophet.

> *"For unto us a child is born, unto us a son is given... He was despised and rejected by men, a man of sorrows, and familiar with suffering...Surely he took up our infirmities and carried our sorrows...But he was pierced for our transgressions, he was crushed for our iniquities; the punishment that brought us peace was upon him, and by his wounds we are healed."*
> *Isaiah 9:6, 53: 3, 4, 5*

So what happened with this prophecy of healing? How did God implement His plan of redemption? What delivered His chosen ones from such horrific consequences of the original falling to the temptation?

We read in Hebrews and Romans:

> *"Let us fix our eyes on Jesus, the author and perfecter of our faith, who for the joy set before him endured the cross, scorning its shame, and sat down at the right hand of the throne of God." Hebrews 12:2*

" As the Scripture says, Everyone who trusts in him
will never be put to shame."Romans 10:11

It is finished. The day Jesus arrived into your life, the day He became your Lord, your shame was taken care of. As one writer expressed it, "He approached us tenderly in our shame-filled failure, forgiving us our perpetual sin... our longing to be like God... our longing to be in control... of the universe."[4]

Let me remind you of two scenes. You know them well. The response to the woman brought by the shamers to Jesus. They were shaming her for her adultery, and remember why they were doing this. They were setting up Jesus, to shame him. So Jesus was encountering intentional, deliberate shaming. And what does Jesus do? He pauses to have them reflect on their own lives... and says, as the shamers slink away,

> *"Woman, where are those thine accusers? hath no*
> *one condemned thee?"...Neither do I condemn thee:*
> *go, and sin no more." John 8:10 (The King James*
> *Version)*

His ministry was typified by extending forgiveness. Remember the four men lowering the paralyzed man through the roof of the house where Jesus was teaching. Their impressive pursuit of healing prompted by faith was totally successful. He extended forgiveness to the shameful sinfulness of the impaired, paralyzed by sin and the accompanying shame.

> *"When Jesus saw their faith, he said to the paralytic,*
> *'Son, your sins are forgiven'."Mark 2:5*

Jesus was ministering to shame-filled hearts where he was given access. But his access was sometimes denied by those in leadership in Israel. The Pharisees, virtually the pillars of the synagogue, were totally focused on their deeds. They claimed righteousness based on their ability to keep the laws. They refused to look inward.

> *"The Pharisee stood up and prayed about himself:*
> *'God, I thank you that I am not like all other men—*
> *robbers, evildoers, adulterers—or even like this tax*
> *collector. I fast twice a week and give a tenth of all I*
> *get."Luke 18:11-12*

They denied God access to their hearts. Notice the pharisaical avoidance of their hearts, the focus on deeds, contrasted with the vulnerability of the Psalmist:

> *"Search me, O God, and know my heart! Try me and*
> *know my thoughts. And see if there be any wicked way*
> *in me, and lead me in the way everlasting" Psalm*
> *139:23-4 (The Revised Standard Version)*

Could it be that their refusal to look inward was a defense against shame? The disciples were warned about the hypocrisy of the Pharisees. Perhaps the terror of encountering shame closed and hardened the hearts of these Pharisees, creating their hypocrisy. And, we too, want to stay focused on our outward behavior.

> *"Woe to you, teachers of the law and Pharisees, you hypocrites! You clean the outside of the cup and dish, but inside they are full of greed and self-indulgence. Blind Pharisee! First clean the inside of the cup and dish, and then the outside also will be clean."Matthew 23:25-6*

These pillars of the synagogue were refusing to acknowledge the sinful nature inherent in man since the fall, when Adam and Eve reached from finiteness trying to become infinite. And, we too, crave to have that sinful nature and finiteness not be true about us. And what we do to avoid having those things be exposed actually creates far more misery than if we faced our sinful nature and our finiteness.

Face what? Face our capacities for revenge, for jealousy, for envy, face our desire to call the shots, face our craving to make the uncertain, certain. We want to be in control, we want to make this come out right. I want to stay safe. I want to look good, I want to look on top of my game. I don't want to settle for being finite. I want to be infinite. And I've got to get in control, if I'm going to succeed in these determinations.

The irony is that God's plan requires the opposite of our denial, our secrecy about our finiteness and our sinful nature. By facing and acknowledging those tendencies and those capacities, they become manageable. Then the Holy Spirit within us can begin to manage the inventory of our deceitful hearts. Only by owning our finiteness and our sinful nature, can they be submitted to God.

So this part of our nature that we all share in common is categorized as innate shame. We experience innate shame regarding our sinful nature and our finiteness. Shame hides these unacceptable capacities and creates vulnerability for a shame attack when any of these shame-laden tendencies are released from storage. And in this hidden state, these capacities are not available to God. They are not available for the transforming work of the Holy Spirit.

So let us press on to understand the other categories of shame stored away, usually hidden from our own awareness. Understanding the particular origin of the shame we experience in a shame attack can be an important part of the healing process. In the next chapter we will consider the category of shame called existential shame.

Chapter 3

Existential Shame

"Today you are you! That is truer than true!

There is no one alive who is you-er than you! [1]

Theodor Seuss Geisel and Audrey S. Geisel

It was 1945. Our country was celebrating the end of a war that had taken many lives of America's finest. One woman, an exception to the hellacious effect of war, blessed with a beautiful 4-year-old daughter, now had her husband home from the war. And now she was delighted to discover that their second child was on the way. They, like so many other families they knew, were adjusting to a blessed time of peace and optimistically looking toward their future. Times were good. And in these good times, this mother began to prepare the beautiful brown-haired, brown-eyed little darling for the arrival of a sibling. Her desire to round out her family with a baby boy became more intense as the delivery date approached. Because this was before medical science had developed the sonogram technique, she was not given the choice to know the gender of the child she was preparing to deliver. Nevertheless, her heart, deceived by an obsessive desire, drove her to begin to speak of the arrival of a son.

Somewhere in those last days of waiting, her desire crossed a fine line and became an obsession. She arrived at the hospital and labored through until the miracle of life was announced by the attending physician, speaking loudly to get a decibel above the first wails of a newborn. "It's a girl, and she looks and sounds great."

In the next few moments, this woman's excited, exhausted anticipation took a nose dive. She plunged into disappointment, anger, and self pity. For the next three days, this precious little newborn would not be held by her mother. She would not be cuddled and stroked. She would not bring awe to the woman in whose womb she had been nourished for nine months. She would not have her mother's eyes intently making contact with her own little blue eyes. This mother refused to let the nurses bring this innocent little newborn to her. And on the day of discharge, would remark about the blue eyes and the shock of blond hair as such an ugly baby. This innocent little miracle began to experience shame. Her mother's refusal to meet the newborn's basic needs of a tender, love-filled touch and a tender voice were not being met. Instead she was being shamed. She was experiencing existential shame. She was being shamed with the non-verbal message, "You are not what I wanted. It is not good that you are here."

So we are looking at the second category of shame, existential shame. The innate shame described in the previous chapter is a universal part of our nature as human beings. Existential shame has to do with the conditions or circumstances of our very early life, that were in fact shaming. Experts who have studied existential shame recount three types of existential shame.

The first one regards a rupture or interruption in the mother/child relationship of a physical nature. For varied reasons, the newborn and mother are not able to have quality time to begin creating that much needed bond. We refer to that as a rupture in the child/parent relationship. Occasionally the rupture is a choice from a deceived heart such as the account cited at the beginning of the chapter. But more often such neglect of a newborn is completely out of human control due to medical conditions. And this situation brings much sympathy to the newborn and the parents. Sometimes the heartache and angst of the mother over this causes denial. Even though the lack of bonding was not the mother's fault, it still damages a child. It is a shaming experience for the newborn. Fortunately it seems that the present generation of medical staff and parents are much more in tune with the need for the newborn and the mother to have quality time for their bonding to begin.

In my own family, I am grateful that this need has been understood. Some of my grandchildren have been blessed with parents who were aware and saw to their newborn's need when faced with a challenging situation. They extended creative effort to work around the isolation imposed by the bilirubin blanket required when the baby was jaundiced. We all prayed for lower jaundice numbers, so the cuddling and touching could be sufficient to get the bonding underway, so that their love-filled touch could impart crucial messages of " it is good that you are here, little one".

Of course I cannot ignore in this discussion the reality that sometimes the physical rupture is not unavoidable, such as the story that opened this chapter. We read of an abandoned baby and know if the little one survives physically, there will be a shaming wound from rejection at birth. The baby will experience shame regarding its existence. So these are types of physical existential shame that some of us have endured.

The second type of existential shame involves a rejection that is more psychological than physical. The mother is physically present, meeting the needs of her baby to be fed and cleaned, but failing to convey love to the little one. Again the precious little needy life is getting shamed by not getting the message, "It is good that you're here." I will continue to refer to the primary caregiver as mother. But please know that whoever the primary care giver is, that person needs to send accepting and caring messages. If this person is not doing a good enough job of accepting and caring continually for the child, responding to the child, the child is being shamed. The adequate meeting of those needs begins to help the parents and child form an attachment. But if either of the parents is stressed, or angry, or disappointed with the child, or even preoccupied with issues unrelated to the child, the risk is huge that the child's early attachment needs will not be sufficiently met. And an unmet need is a shamed need. When any of these negative emotions prevail, the child is at risk for concluding, "It is a shame that I am here. It is a shame that I exist."

Bonding is a popular word these days. Bonding depicts the healthy bridge or connection from a parent to child. If that bonding is inadequate or ruptured, automatically the child experiences shame... the sense of "I do not belong", the sense of " I should not be here", "this family would be better off without me", "it is not good that I am". The child draws these conclusions based on needs not being met. We will look in detail at other needs of a child in the next chapter.

Of course these negative messages are the total opposite of what God said. It's totally opposite of His description of making each of us wonderfully, of calling each of us by name, of having a plan for each of our lives.

> *"For you created my inmost being; you knit me together in my mother's womb. I praise you, because I am fearfully and wonderfully made; your works are wonderful, I know that full well." Psalm 139: 13-14*

> *"The Lord called me from the womb, from the body of my mother he named my name." Isaiah 49:1 (Revised Standard Version).*

"For I know the plans I have for you, says the Lord, plans for welfare and not for evil, to give you a future and a hope." Jeremiah 29: 11 (Revised Standard Version).

There are some very powerful stories coming forth now, from either the mother or the child about conception in rape. Popular Christian writer, speaker, Lee Ezell tells in her book, *The Missing Piece,* of her brutal rape at age 18, that resulted in pregnancy.[2] Refusing a "friend's" offer for a ride to Mexico for an abortion, she carried her daughter to term and released her for adoption.

More than twenty years later, Lee Ezell's daughter Julie, also an inspiring speaker, readily admits, "Yes, I am the result of rape, but I am so glad I did not get the death penalty for the crime of my father! After all, it doesn't matter how you begin in life, but what you become."[3] Julie would find her birth mother. Their poignant and powerful reunion affirms God's value and purpose invested in each of us, regardless of the conditions of our conception. Their story plunges us into the reality that there is no such thing as a human being that is a mistake. A surprise maybe, but not a mistake.

Families and/or communities may look at a conception as a mistake. Theologically, there is no such thing. Theologically, no one arrives on this planet without having been knit together in their mother's womb, known by name, and a future planned for by our Creator. We will come back to this issue of bonding later when we explore the concept of attachment. For a child needs to begin life with consistent bonding experiences with the parents and continue an attachment to the parents as an older baby, a toddler, a preschooler, and on into adulthood.

The third type of shame that I classify as existential is a specific shaming dynamic called "being made into a tool". One of the renowned experts on shame believes this to be one of the most damaging ways that a child can be shamed.[4] This dynamic can be deceiving because of its subtlety.

Being made into a tool refers to parents' using a child for their own fantasy, purposes or intentions. Kaufman describes that the child's existence is used for another's personal fulfillment. This use entails the complete disregard of the child as a person in his own right. The parent using the child does not convey to the child that she has her destiny apart from the parent. The child has no way of knowing that the Creator has a unique plan for him or her. In other words, the message that is coming across from the significant adult to the child is "I exist for another's dreams, intentions, purposes." So that the existence of a person in his or her own right is not honored, and is therefore shamed. Psychiatrist, C.G. Jung states, "Nothing has a stronger influence psychologically on their environment and especially on their children than the unlived life of the parent."[5]

This attitude on the part of the using parent is considered a form of contempt. The contemptuous message that the child is receiving is that his feelings, his needs, and his preferences do not count. Only the adult's designs determine what the child can and will be. So the child is a victim. The child is a used person, used as merely a means, not recognized as an end unto himself. The following examples will probably ring very familiar. One is a classic – the one we call the stage mother. We may be most familiar with it regarding celebrities. However some of you will recognize it as a part of your childhood, perhaps on a smaller scale. This is where the stage mother pushes and cajoles and manipulates the child into performing in some way, typically the performing arts. It is obvious to onlookers that this is for the needs of the mother. Her intense involvement, her overly zealous involvement speaks loudly as to her motivation. It is not for the needs of the child. It is meeting a deep personal need of the mother.

Let us remember an important given at this point. For every child, the parent is always right, at least at the unconscious level. The child is totally dependent on these big people and cannot entertain the notion that either of them could be failing significantly in their parenting. The child's security would be threatened if a parent were perceived as using poor judgment, stuck in a parenting pattern that was a huge mistake. On a conscious level a child may disapprove or disagree with something done by the parent. But at the same time, unconsciously, the child is assuming the ultimate blame for the shame being experienced.

Now we will not let the dads get off scot-free in this discussion. Where can you see it in the dads? How about a little league game? Go to the little league game, and here is the red flag. (No pun intended.) When you see a father who is excessively emotional, overly invested in the child's performance, in the child's winning, in the child's playing superbly, there is a good chance that the father is attempting to get some of his own needs met, through the child's performance. Watch him pace up and down the boundary line of the playing field. Hear him yelling at the coach, at the refs, or at his child. Is his child a person in his own right or is his child an extension of the father? Is this his second chance with his own dreams and ambitions?

A variation on this theme of being made into a tool is a dynamic referred to as parentification.[6] When parents' childhood needs for empathy, understanding, and a sense of being cared for were not sufficiently met and, therefore shamed, they often seek the experience of being cared for by their own child.[7] This reversal of the parent-child role shames the child's need to be cared for by making the parent's need the only one of importance. The parentified child frequently enters adulthood strongly programmed to attend to another's need to be cared for, no longer able to experience his or her own need. The shaming of this legitimate childhood need and its usual consequences is one way we see the development of codependency.

So these are the classic examples of these types of existential shame. These shaming dynamics bring to mind the well-known parental instruction in the Bible.

"Train up a child in the way he should go, and when he is old, he will not depart from it." Proverbs 22:6 (The Revised Standard Version)

Notice that the focus is on the way the child should go, on the child's need, not the unfulfilled need of a parent. The child has been invested with abilities, interests, dreams, and potential that are uniquely his. When these investments are not identified, much less developed, much of who God created him to be is shamed.

At this point, when presenting this material in a seminar, I show one of my favorite cartoons that I fondly entitled "The Bradshaw Bears". You can see the outline of two bears hanging out in the woods, one complaining to the other: "His name's Bradshaw. He says he understands I came from a single parent den with inadequate role models. He senses that my dysfunctional behavior is shame based and codependent and he urges me to let my inner cub heal. I say we eat him". This lighter moment is offered in case you may be beginning to feel weary. Perhaps the proverbial light at the end of the tunnel is not appearing soon enough. You may be longing for a positive uplifting turn. God's heart may hold more hope for healing for you than you can muster right now.

So let me encourage you to stay the course. Remember something good this way comes because His trustworthy promises usher us toward the abundant life.

Chapter 4

Personal Shame

"Fathers, do not exasperate your children; instead, bring them up in the training and instruction of the Lord." Ephesians 6:4

*I*n the novel, *Of Human Bondage*, nine-year-old Philip was sent to boarding school by his uncle, now his guardian because Philip had suffered the death of both parents. The school soon evolves into a place of torment for young Philip. The specific object of the scorn by his classmates is Philip's clubfoot. The first time on the playground, his handicap causes nothing but clumsiness and prevents him from being able to tag any of the boys. Soon all the boys are mockingly limping and screaming in high pitched merriment. The next scene of torment would ensue that night in the dormitory. Philip refuses the snide request to see his foot. Ultimately three boys physically attack a horrified Philip, creating a demand for him to stick his foot out from under the covers. The ridicule continues as one of them touches it with the tip of one finger, curiously

tracing the outline of the deformity. The appearance of the head-
master sends each tormentor to his own bed. The author says this:
"He was crying not for the pain they had caused him, nor for the
humiliation he had suffered when they looked at his foot, but with
rage at himself because, unable to stand the torture, he had put out
his foot of his own accord."[1] The shame surrounding the uncovering
of his deformity was intensified by his perception of having contributed to his own humiliation. We are now to personal shame, the
third and final category of shame. This last category becomes more
personal in that the shaming we experience is directly about some
shameful part of us. Therefore this type of shaming is categorized as
personal shame. Although the lack of adequate bonding described
in the previous chapter can be more existential in nature, we will
examine the dynamic of bonding, or attachment, more closely in this
chapter regarding personal shame.

Charles Whitfield's list of universal needs, Table 4.1, "A
Hierarchy of Human Needs", specifies the needs that every child
arrives with at birth.[2] Once we become familiar with these basic
needs, we can begin to take note of whether our needs were met sufficiently. We can evaluate how a need was met by seeing it on a continuum. (At one end of the continuum needs are not met at all. At the
other end needs are excellently met.) Mental health professionals
have adopted a perspective that avoids requiring perfection in parenting. And so they think in terms of *good enough*. Turn now and read
Table 4.1. Since the Table 4.1 items are self-explanatory, I will limit

my comments to a few of them. Notice how no. 10, "Acceptance" has several facets to it. Each of them is important though there is some overlap among these facets. But taken all together, these facets present a good description of the actions that make a child feel accepted. A foundational theme found in "Acceptance" is that the child is known. Curt Thompson, emphasizes in, *Anatomy of the Soul*, the necessity of being known, ultimately to experience being known by God.[3] Other themes in "Acceptance" include feeling respected in all aspects of who you are. The culmination of this kind of parenting is that children have a sense of belonging. Children who experience this parental acceptance feel loved. Another need in Table 4.1, no. 11 "Opportunity to grieve losses and to grow," is specific regarding the particular feeling of grief resulting from loss.

Often in my office, I have the privilege of walking with someone, who feels shame, into the shame of their life regarding losses. Rarely does that walk reveal that the significant adults in our life have adequately helped us cope with this experience of loss. The mishandling of loss fails to help a child grow in his confidence that he can get through the pain of loss. Grief can feel like no end in sight. Especially is this true if no one is there to share in the grief with us. Our youngest daughter was 8 years old when a beloved grandparent died. We gave our children an opportunity to go to the hospital to say good bye to their dear grandmother. Our 8-year-old wanted to go. She tearfully whispered a wrenching goodbye to her semi-comatose grandmother saying, "I'll see you in heaven." She attended the funeral and the burial. We all cried together. Even so, she remembers thinking, "I'll always be this sad, for the rest of my life." My paternal grandmother was widowed when my father was 10 years old. My father's pain was visible as he told me that his mother stood as the last shovel of dirt went on her husband's grave, brushed her hands, and said, "And that's the end of that." References to his father were few and far between after that agonizing loss.

Others report very little explanation from parents when a loved one was terminally ill. They received minimum disclosure about a death and sound bite size references to the deceased forever afterward. The need to grieve and to have our grief validated is appropriate. Frequently approval of our particular way of grieving is met quite insufficiently. And to the extent that need is not met, it is shamed. And so we experience shame regarding grief. The suffering that comes with death, or any loss, is compounded when the need to grieve is shamed. Thereafter any loss throughout a lifetime carries the potential of stirring up the shame that became associated with loss. Continuing with Table 4.1, no. 14, "Accomplishment" speaks to the way our tasks were handled. The important adults in our life need to balance support and challenge, terms used by Gary Sibcy in *Parenting Today's Kids*.[4] This is the delicate act of tight rope-walking. Not only is it important to challenge a child with a task but also to step in with assistance at the moment that support is needed. This dynamic helps determine how a child grows into being able to say with the titled character in *The Little Engine That Could*, "I think I can." Parents who overprotect are imbalanced with too much support and not enough challenge. This overprotective parenting can send a message that the child is not competent. Currently such hovering over a child is referred to as helicopter parenting.

Parents who leave a child too much on its own are imbalanced with too much challenge and not enough support. Perhaps you have noticed the teaching style in elementary school is to encourage children to get their thoughts on paper – never mind the spelling. I think I caught on to this approach in time to not impinge on my grandchildren's sense of accomplishment by overlooking the misspelled words. Also in this arena of accomplishment is the importance of encouraging a child's creativity. And so we have learned to admire the little ones' unrecognizable application of paint to paper with awe, by requesting, "Tell me about it".

No. 16, "Sexuality" in Table 4.1 covers a wide range of needs. A child needs to experience that the significant adults in his life are content with their gender, as well as content with the child's gender. A child needs positive preparation for puberty and a respectful attitude conveyed to him about human sexuality. The attitudes that the marital sexual relationship was a duty of the woman or the only interest of a man may be gone with the wind—and good riddance. Such attitudes were examples of shaming God's creation of sexuality. It is to be hoped that the current generation of parents have enough of the perspective from the "Song of Solomon" to convey a healthy, Godly view of sexuality to their children. But many of previous generations grew up with significant shame attached to their sexuality. And so the delight in our sexuality that oozes from the Bible is just wishful thinking for many generations. Or perhaps our sexuality has so much shame attached to it that it would be felt as shameful to desire that kind of delight. Bring on the healing! (Sexual abuse will be discussed later in this chapter.)

Continuing with no. 17, "Enjoyment or fun" may seem rather obvious. However the following moment is not unusual in my office. A very responsible, well-groomed, successful woman has been bravely tackling some problem areas in her life for several sessions. She is pleased with some changes she has made. And now she makes a shift in her focus. The shift stirs a little anxiety. I am alert for the possibility that shame may be stirring within her. Tersely the forbidden comes out of her mouth. "I have been thinking that I just don't know how to have fun." There. She has said it. And we will begin to notice the shame stirred by the desire to simply have more fun. When I am presenting this material, the audience always relates to the dynamic of having laughter and playfulness shamed by someone. This shuts down their delight. Or in the absence of specific memories, they are aware that they are programmed for "all work and no play". And they laugh aloud when I ask this rhetorical question: "Were they afraid that we would get so wound up that we would just orbit right off the earth?"

Finally no. 20, "Unconditional love" really is embedded in all of the other 19 needs. My cousin and I had teenagers in the same era. And so we commiserated over the worrisome choices they were making on what seemed like a regular basis. I gratefully recall sharing my angst with her. On one occasion we reaped the benefit of coming to a profound conclusion regarding our parenting. And it went like this: "Well, even if he ends up in jail, I'll go visit him." It seemed as if we had worked our way through our worries sufficiently to conclude what unconditional love would mean for us. Notice in Table 4.1 that connecting with a Higher Power is included in no. 20, serving as another reminder to "...bring them up in the training and instruction of the Lord."

Table 4.1, "A Hierarchy of Human Needs" listed the needs of children. What are the actions or attitudes found in parents, schools, or churches, which hinder children from receiving the nurturing, healthful messages? In Table 4.2, Dr. Whitfield outlines a list of rules that often typify a family, church, or school that abides by shaming rules, as well as a list of messages the children may be receiving[5]. The lists are not exhaustive. Let us examine Table 4.2 that follows and apply this material to our experiences. We may add to the list or modify certain items to be more representative of the traditions in our families or our communities.

Another way of understanding how shame may have been ushered into our being is through the concept of attachment. The theory or paradigm called attachment has been used in various modalities since its inception. John Bowlby, who is credited with launching attachment theory, is quoted by Clinton and Sibcy in *Attachments*.

"Unthinking confidence in the unfailing accessibility and support of attachment figures is the bedrock on which stable and self-reliant personality is built."[6]

While our focus is on the issue of attachment for the young child, attachment is a well respected issue throughout one's lifetime. For example, the work of Leslie Greenberg and Susan Johnson sees attachment as the core issue in the paradigm they developed for marital therapy. A major theme in their paradigm is that a strong marital attachment creates a secure base from which one confidently goes out to meet the challenges of life. Greenberg and Johnson included the research built on Gottman and others to build a successful methodology for helping couples break distancing patterns that assault their marital attachment[7]

To return to our focus on shame as an internal response to unmet needs – let us consider a baby's need for attachment. So if we look again at Table no. 4.1, we see the specifics of how caregivers or parents develop this bond called attachment with their baby. For example, needs listed as no. 3-5, "Touching, skin contact, Attention, Mirroring and echoing" flow well with the following comment from the attachment literature. It suggests that for a baby, "being lovingly held is the greatest spur to development," noting that "...the mother's autonomic nervous system in effect communicates with her baby's nervous system soothing it through touch [and that] withholding close bodily contact accounted for anxious and avoidant behavior patterns."[8]

The field of neuroscience has been exploding with scientific evidence, using brain scans, to observe the activated areas in the brain produced in our experience of emotions. And so the psychological perspective gained by utilizing analyses of brain scans and chemical reactions produces interesting outcomes, which include an enhancement of how we understand attachment.[9] The patterns of attachment, called styles, that developed in our tender years tend to form a pattern for the way we will attach or relate to another in adulthood.

Three of the four styles reflect attachment injuries or failures of the caregivers to meet the needs of an infant. As you can see in Table 4.3, "Attachment Styles"[10], the first style described is the *good enough* one called "Secure Attachment Style." Before we look further at the types of styles, let's look at the needs of a child described in attachment theory. In Table 4.4[11] are 4 simple questions – simple in their wording, profound in their meaning. I have often said that a baby makes its debut in this world with a question stamped on its forehead – "Am I loveable?" As the theory of attachment has developed, I have added one more question to the stamped forehead. And the additional question has to do with others – can I trust those around me for support? So the four questions listed in table 4.4 embody the crucial needs of experiencing self as worthy of being loved and competent to get the love that is needed and experiencing others as reliable, trustworthy, accessible, and willing to respond when needed. As one author states, "Unfortunately not all babies and their parents establish a warm empathetic way of being together that would eventually enable the child to step confidently in the wider world."[12]. It is indeed unfortunate and shaming when a child cannot answer the questions in Table 4.4 with "yes, good enough". Table 4.5[13] describes how the shaming can transpire. Five general descriptive categories are outlined regarding when the caregiver is not sufficiently responsive and attuned. These situations also refer to distancing or anti-attachment behaviors among adults. These needs are incredibly foundational and crucial. So much so that the child's personality is directly and profoundly impacted. The shame that is created by these unmet needs is in proportion to the lack of responsiveness and attunement the baby experiences. Table 4.6, "Personality Traits Corresponding to Attachment Styles," gives a brief summary of how the personality is impacted by shamed needs, creating particular personality traits. The quotes about Mum are from one of the British writers.[14] As indicated earlier, childhood sexual abuse needs to be emphasized for traumatizing in a way that introduces shame at a deep level.[15] These quoted authors continue to explain. "The lingering impact of the toxic shame of sexual abuse can paralyze people with distorted beliefs that they somehow actually invited the abuse or at least failed to stop it. Again, distorted identity is in play here, and people hear their internal voice saying, 'I am a failure; I am dirty; I am damaged goods.' External shameful abuse has become internal shameful identity."

So the verbal and emotional abuse we examined in the Tables in this chapter, physical abuse, and profoundly sexual abuse, all scar a person's sense of self and its worth. Incest is a particularly wicked type of sexual abuse that perpetrates shame to the innocent child's core. The accumulation of these scars may create a shaming belief that declares one unworthy of anyone's love, time or attention. The final focus for this chapter is on the possible potential parts of us that have been shamed. In other words, what might be the specific outcomes of unmet needs, growing up in an environment of shaming rules and messages, suffering attachment injuries, and/or victimized by abuse. This outline, Table 4.7, "Potential for Shame", begins with community and family shame before going on to propose potential specifics of personal shame.

Later when we examine the guidelines for healing, this outline will be suggested as a reference. Table 4.7 is a focus on the possible results of a child's needs going unmet. It is the "so what" of having encountered shame, especially in the young and tender years. Turn now and examine Table 4.7. Often we don't remember the actual experiences whereby a specific part of us was shamed. (My use of the word "part" is meant to convey an actual body part or a characteristic, or a behavior – ANYTHING about us. (The use of the word "part" also includes something that was done to us such as being abused or something shameful associated with us.) Frequently those painful experiences were long ago exiled from our conscious memory. Fortunately the healing that awaits us is not dependent on our conscious memory of actual shaming incidents.

One type of shame that we as individuals often feel comes *not* from our own actions. This shame is non-personal — it is derived from the perspectives of other people—and is thus called "borrowed shame". As one author explains, the term "borrowed" shame keeps the focus on returning shame to its original owner. Returning borrowed shame, one way of reducing our shame, involves letting others take responsibility for the shame they harbor within.[16] This is the shame that can envelop an entire community. For example, we may feel shame when we hear degrading statements about our culture, our race, or even our way of speaking. (I can remember the moment that my southern ears first heard the term "mush-mouth" in reference to southern drawls. Fortunately I was well beyond my tender years and the shame embodied in that term had minimal impact on me.) Whether we come from the north or the south, the country or the city, the wrong side of the tracks, or a ritzy neighborhood—the potential is there for other people to degrade us and cause shame that can even become characteristic of our entire community. We can reduce our feeling of shame by returning the responsibility for harboring disparaging ideas to those who have harbored and expressed degrading opinions about us.

And then there is the type of borrowed shame that merely envelops our family. A family may have had characteristics that someone deemed shameful such as poverty. But shame is not necessarily attached to poverty. No doubt you have heard people tell stories of how poor they were, and they never knew it... wonderful stories of how families lived in poverty, but did not allow it to become a shameful issue for the family.

Other family potential for shame may be whether your family members were sufficiently educated, acceptably employed, free of scandal, of the customary religion, had a member with a chronic illness or handicap. Who put the rule book together that says, "be ashamed because a family member's epilepsy brings on grand mal seizures in public?" Who put the rule book together that deems some condition shameful that our family must bear? For example, acceptable employment can be a requirement to be a professional or a requirement to continue the family tradition of being a blue collar worker and to do otherwise would be to "get above your raising". It really does not matter. Families can carry shame around any issue.

Emotional illness is common ground for shame. The classic clue that shame abounds around an issue is the secrecy that surrounds it. So if we discover that we know very little about a relative or an issue of a particular relative, chances are someone deemed that person or that issue shameful and others have gone along with that judgment. It is not uncommon for a flabbergasting truth to emerge about a relative whose very existence was secreted in shame.

Then of course, common issues such as a child conceived out of wedlock, divorce, addiction, too religious, or not religious enough are all grist for the shaming mill. Any traits of a family can make the shame list. Anything can be shamed. Can you feel the arbitrariness of what gets labeled shameful? Now we move on to the third section of Table 4.7, "Personal". Notice the core principle in the first comment of this table. An unmet need is a shamed need.

We start considering personal shame by thinking about our body. When we are growing up, we began to notice some people have a fat body, some people have a skinny body, some people are tall, some are short, some people have course hair, and some people have thin hair. Suddenly these bodily characteristics begin to be weighed and evaluated by the family or by others outside our family. And in the weighing, someone tips the scale so that something about our body gets shamed. (Many people are trying to counter the influence that celebrities have on young girls regarding unrealistic standards for body image.)

So as many body parts as we have, there is the potential for shame. There's the sense of, oops I just do not make it. And it can go either way. Oh, my gosh, everybody in the family has beautiful black raven hair, and here I am, a blond. This is unacceptable, or vice versa is unacceptable. You get the feel of what this is all about. Who set up the rule book as to what trait is acceptable, and what trait is unacceptable?

The body... it goes on and on. The bodily functions... has anybody ever not been shamed for peeing in their pants? How does anybody get through childhood without an incident of shame around normal body functions? And then, moving on into puberty. What girl gets into young womanhood without some shame around her bodily development or its monthly functions? What young man gets to adulthood without having erections and wet dreams shamed?

How about movements of the body? Are you coordinated? Was your family athletic? If our family was athletic, we had better not be uncoordinated. How about too athletic? Maybe our family was scholarly and they spent a lot of time in books and so shame might be delivered in the question "...another ball game? You've got good books on your shelf that have not even been opened". It does not matter. It is entirely arbitrary. If people carry shame about a particular part of us, we are going to get shamed.

What about your voice? Were you too loud? Did you laugh too much? "You're a cackling hyena. You just need to calm down. Too much laughter is not lady-like!"

How about posture? Did the way you carried yourself reap shame for you?

How about your smile? How about the lack of smile? "You don't smile enough. Don't show your gums when you smile."

Mannerisms of any sort are up for shame. "Look at the way you walk. Could you just put one foot in front of the other... and point your toes ahead... can't you do better than that?" Now we move our focus from our body to our emotions, starting with excitement/joy.

Look again at Table 4.2. Certainly one of the common practices of shaming is listed as no. 1. "Don't express your feelings." Most people arrive in my office knowing they want to develop better management of their emotions. They struggle with having emotions that to them are unacceptable. Ultimately the meaning of these undesirable feelings is that they are bad people. Can you sense the shame that is being uncovered as we follow this train of thought? So shame has become wrapped around certain emotions. (In the world of neuroscience, we would speak of neurons firing together until they are wired together.) So when shame is bound with a feeling, some degree of shame will be felt along with that shame-bound feeling. When shame is wired to a feeling, such as anger was for me, we do not own it. And an unowned feeling can be likened to a loose cannon in our motivations and behaviors. The issue is what those feelings motivate us to do. Or the more crucial issue is what we actually do due to having certain emotions. Most of us were not taught to identify what we were feeling, much less our options of how to manage the feelings that well up within us.

I have already mentioned excitement/joy. Did you get too excited as a child? Did somebody need to calm you down? After all,.. " life is serious business. Life is a vale of tears. Don't be so silly. That is not that funny. Calm down. Stop fooling around. Enough is enough." Did you ever hear these shaming admonitions?

The excitement and the joy that spontaneously and exuberantly comes forth from us is a likely target for shame. It is almost as if a fear prevailed that we would go right into adulthood, turning cartwheels down the center aisle of the church... if most of our excitement/joy were not shamed out of us.

So the impact of sustaining significant shame around our excitement/joy is that by the time we are adults, we will use shame to calm down our own excitement. For example, as we discover a better way to do a certain task, such as my discovery that my word processor capitalizes the first letter of a sentence. Anything that improves the way we do a task, that carries a spark of joy–how long does it last? How long do we celebrate a blessing that comes our way? Can we hold the thought, "That is so neat, I'll never have to do it the old way again". How soon after the discovery do we go... "duh!!!" ... smack our palm to our forehead and render the shaming scorn of, " Finally!! You've only been working with that program for eight months."

We so naturally attenuate our excitement and joy. In fact one of the experts thinks that the major use of shame is to manage these emotions that otherwise can create a sense of being out of control[17]. Thus we rain on our own parade. Never mind what other people do to us when there is joy and excitement brewing. "Don't count your chickens before they hatch." We have wonderful reasons for joy and excitement often. But we don't allow the full experience of that spark of joy that wells up within us. Think about attempting to compliment someone with "good job." Instead of allowing a shared moment of pleasure, we may hear, "Oh, it could have been better." And this management of pleasure is frequently defended with "I don't want to get prideful, to get a big-head, to get too big for my britches." Do any of those fears seem familiar?

And this creates a segue into what is the most frequently identi- fied shaming comment. It is a question, but it is a rhetorical question. "Who do you think you are?" You may never have heard the words, but the look, the body language, we have all heard it. It comes across one way or another. Is there anybody who has never thought, even for a moment, regarding a dream, a potential achievement, a thought of "maybe I could do... or maybe I could be...", and never had it quickly followed with that very shaming thought ... "Who do you think you are?"

Another frequently shamed emotion is anxiety. When some of us became anxious, we were accused of worrying over nothing. "You're too moody, what's the matter, cat got your tongue?" If my worry, my anxiousness is not acceptable, it soon becomes shameful and gets disowned. Especially do little boys get shamed for being a fraidy cat.

And, then, of course, there is anger. My most disowned emotion was clearly anger. Growing up in the Bible Belt in a Christian community didn't bode well for me to know that anger was God-given and useful. So when Sarah didn't show up for basketball practice I was angry because our team needed her. My father took care to make sure that my anger got stuffed, never to be expressed which, no doubt, would have reaped him serious shame. Since this represented a pattern in our household, I reached adulthood emotionally handicapped. My own children labor hard to be able to know me and connect with me in my anger.

How well do we manage sadness? How about our tears? Did anybody ever get permission to be tearful when growing up? Or did you get, "Stop that or I'll give you something to cry about"?

And even today, look at what we say when we talk about our tears. What are the expressions we use? "I lost it." What do you mean, you lost it? Your sanity? Your wallet? You lost what? It is such a negative description of having cried about something. Or another expression is "I broke down." You broke down? Something is broken? You had tears, but something is broken? Think about it. Let us stop doing that. We can start a campaign. Let us just learn to say, that brought tears to my eyes. I cried about that. I cried hard and heavy. I sobbed. Let us respect ourselves, our sadness, and our tears instead of shaming these God-given emotions.

So those are some of the emotions and the ways they get shamed. And then they are ultimately disowned because experiencing them is not worth the painful shame that became wired with them. The pain of shame when a certain emotion wells up within causes us to repress the emotion instead of experiencing it.

How about the drives lodged in the nature of human beings, two of which are listed in Table 4.7. The sexual drive is listed first due to the enormous amount of shame about it in many cultures and families. For example, how about "Good girls don't flirt". Or how about all the shame men are subject to around their sexual drive? Even today I hear a glimmer of shame when someone talks about men being visual, that they are sexually aroused visually–quicker and easier than a woman. Most of the time, I hear comments from women about this part of God's design in men that are conveyed in a tone of shame. It implies shame on men that visual stimulation is arousing for them. Since that's a part of God's design, how do we justify disapproving of or shaming this feature of masculine sexuality?

The other drive listed is hunger. How about comments such as, "You can't be hungry, we just ate." Or there is the shaming response, "What? You don't like my cooking? Not good enough for you?" Some of us had some rigid rules about being hungry. We had to be hungry at the right time, for the right food, for the right amount to avoid getting shamed. Have any of us ever NOT been there?

The next category is called "Interpersonal needs". How many of us were coached to express these needs that are listed in Table 4.7? One of my daughters developed an effective way of helping her daughters get her attention. Since she had four little girls under age four, she was likely to need a cue from them. So she taught them this simple request. "I need a moment." I not only appreciate this for my grandchildren, I think we adults would do well to make this request of loved ones. Many of us are just learning to say, "I need a hug," because we were refused a lap when we were seeking comfort as a child. In that shaming moment, I doubt that any of us explained, " I have an interpersonal need right now to be held by you. Please don't shame my need by pushing me away."

How about the need to differentiate? So the family goes to baseball games Saturday afternoons, and I just want to work on my chemistry. Will that be dealt with without my different desire getting shamed? Similarly is the need to identify. "Hey dad, I've got a tie just like yours, I'm just like you dad." "Oh, no. Don't be like me, son." This might be justified as humility. But the child's God-designed need to identify is getting shamed.

How about the need for affirmation? One of my daughters has always been especially gifted and interested in creating with her hands. She forms an idea of a craft and then executes it with amazing skill and artistry. We have talked about my failure to sufficiently affirm this part of who she is. It is no secret that sitting at her craft table soon becomes more like a punishment for me than the pleasure it is for her and my grandchildren. (This example is meant to explain, not to justify, my failure.) Frequently we are too caught up in our own lives to notice another's need. When a friend/colleague updated me about having conquered a challenging computer program, she responded to my response by gently letting me know that she was expecting some "oohs and aahs ". (My preoccupation with my own computer struggles had prevailed.) The ability to express needs is tantamount to strong relationships. Then when we feel the shame of an unmet need and speak up to that effect, the other has an opportunity to repair the wound.

How about the shaming of our intellect? "You are too much of a book worm for this family. We work with our hands." OR... "You're not bookish enough, you just tinker around with that old car all the time. You think too much, you think about things you cannot do anything about, OR if you would just think, put your mind in gear!" Even our capacities for reasoning may be shamed. "You are not being logical. That doesn't make sense. You should have known that was going to happen." Our intellect, our thinking, our remembering, all of that is a likely target with comments such as, "Good thing your head is attached to your body. How could you possibly go to the store for milk, and come home with bread and orange juice? Your glasses are on top of your head, flake! What do you mean, you couldn't find your car? You are hopeless!"

Let us move on to the "Spiritual" category. Maybe when we goofed, when we did something a little less than wonderful, when some finiteness showed up, and we were acknowledging it – perhaps we endured something like, "What will your Sunday School teacher say about that? You had better go to church. You better go to confession. God is watching you, you know." Some of us witnessed religious beliefs getting shamed by the judgment of others as "holier-than-thou" types or the criticism of those who "need a crutch". (Through the years when faith would be likened to a crutch, I would think, "I do not need a crutch, I need a wheel chair." But as life's challenges intensified, my perspective changed. It became apparent to me that God in my life needs to be a gurney, not a crutch, not a wheel chair, but a gurney.)

And then the last category in Table 4.7 is "Purpose". Each of us has a need to know that God has plans in which we are the star. We are dependent on the influential adults in our lives to convey this reality to us. Teachers in particular can play a big role in this need by confidently assuring us that we have a purpose that will reflect our gifts and our creativity. It all goes together. Not only is there a

Godly purpose in our life, but we have been equipped for that purpose. There is creativity, and gifts, and talents already in place for His purposes.

Table 4.7 covers a lot of possibilities. Mark any items that you suspect received a significant amount of shame. This table will be useful when you are in the healing process. Again, this is the heavy part of this book. By now you may be feeling discouraged. Some of us will be recognizing more shaming traditions in our families than we ever imagined. Some of us as parents will know the pain of seeing that we have transferred that shame to the next generation. In spite of our determination to meet needs and be good parents, in spite of wanting better than we had for our children, in spite of doing what we thought to be the right thing, in spite of loving our children deeply and sacrificially, we missed the mark. We missed the mark of meeting some of the needs by the *good enough* standard. We have responded to our children's complaints about our parenting with denial. Their complaints do not seem valid given our intentions to parent them well. The gap between intent and impact can be like the grand canyon. We must take their descriptions of our impact on them seriously. We have to wrestle with that gap in order to promote healing of the shame. We must resolve the mystifying question: How could I have poured my life into my children and still have shamed some of their needs? Hopefully by the end of this book, these realities will be less overwhelming. Rest assured that

God is most interested in healing our shame – both within our own souls, as well as between us and family members.

Table 4.1

A HIERARCHY OF HUMAN NEEDS

1. Survival
2. Safety
3. Touching, skin contact
4. Attention
5. Mirroring and echoing
6. Guidance
7. Listening
8. Being real
9. Participating
10. Acceptance
    - Others are aware of, take seriously and admire the Real You
    - Freedom to be the Real You
    - Tolerance of your feelings
    - Validation
    - Respect
    - Belonging and love
11. Opportunity to grieve losses and to grow
12. Support
13. Loyalty and trust
14. Accomplishment
    - Mastery, "Power," "Control"
    - Creativity
    - Having a sense of completion
    - Making a contribution
15. Altering one's state of consciousness, transcending the ordinary
16. Sexuality
17. Enjoyment or fun
18. Freedom
19. Nurturing
20. Unconditional love (including connection with a Higher Power)

Table 4.2

SHAMING RULES AND MESSAGES

Shaming Rules

1. Don't express your feelings
2. Don't get angry
3. Don't get upset
4. Don't cry
5. Do as I say, not as I do
6. Be good, "nice," perfect
7. Avoid conflict *(or avoid dealing with conflict)*
8. Don't think or talk; just follow directions
9. Do well in school
10. Don't ask questions
11. Don't betray the family with outsiders; keep the family secrets
12. Be seen and not heard!
13. No back talk!
14. Don't contradict me
15. Always look good
16. I'm always right, you're always wrong
17. Always be in control
18. Focus on the troubled person's behavior exclusively
19. Drinking *(or other troubled behavior)* is not the cause of our problems
20. Always maintain the status quo
21. Everyone in the family must be an enabler

Shaming Messages

1. Shame on you
2. You're not good enough
3. I wish I'd never had you
4. Your needs are not all right with me
5. Hurry up and grow up
6. Be dependent
7. Be a man
8. Big boys don't cry
9. Act like a nice girl *(or a lady)*
10. You don't feel that way
11. Don't be like that
12. You're so stupid *(or bad, etc.)*
13. You owe it to us
14. Of course we love you!
15. I'm sacrificing myself for you
16. How can you do this to me?
17. We won't love you if you…
18. You're driving me crazy!
19. You'll never accomplish anything
20. It didn't really hurt
21. You're so selfish
22. You'll be the death of me yet
23. That's not true
24. I promise *(though breaks it)*

ATTACHMENT STYLES

Table 4.3

Secure Attachment Style

Self Dimension
- I am worthy of love.
- I am capable of getting the love and support I need.

Other Dimension
- Others are willing and able to love me.

Ambivalent Attachment Style

Self Dimension
- I am not worthy of love.
- I am not capable of getting the love I need without being angry and clingy.

Other Dimension
- Others are capable of meeting my needs but might not do so because of my flaws.
- Others are trustworthy and reliable but might abandon me because of my worthlessness.

Avoidant Attachment Style

Self Dimension
- I am worthy of love
- I am capable of getting the love and support I need.

Other Dimension
- Others are either unwilling or incapable of loving me.
- Others are not trustworthy; they are unreliable when it comes to meeting my needs.

Disorganized Attachment Style

Self Dimension
- I am not worthy of love.
- I am not capable of getting the love I need without being angry and clingy.

Other Dimension
- Others are unable to meet my needs.
- Others are not trustworthy or reliable.
- Others are abusive, and I deserve it.

Table 4.4

Core Beliefs
The core beliefs that form the self and other dimensions are derived from the following questions:

1. Am *I* worthy of being loved?
2. Am *I* competent to get the love I need?
3. Are *others* reliable and trustworthy?
4. Are *others* accessible and willing to respond to me when I need them to be?

Table 4.5

ATTACHMENT INJURIES

The attachment injuries occur when the caregiver or loved one is not sufficiently near, responsive, and attuned, and instead...

1. ...is simply not available, physically or emotionally due to his or her own emotional distress or discomfort with closeness, e.g. depressed parent.

2. ...is willing to be available but is not able to be there, e.g. parent hospitalized, incapacitated by dealing with the illness, making him / her emotionally unavailable.

3. ...wants to be available and normally would be there but is absent at a crucial developmental phase or a time of crisis, e.g. mother goes back to school when children become teenagers and has little time or energy to help them deal with the turmoil of adolescence

4. ...is there, but instead of providing a safe haven, he or she uses insensitive, off putting, embarrassing, or sarcastic language toward the needy child or adult, e.g. insensitive parent who rebuffs a child when the child gets stressed or a husband who ignores his wife's complaints about her stressful day at work; instead of listening or offering sympathy, he gives unsolicited advice and trivializes her emotional reactions.

5. ...is there but is smothering and overdoes safety and protection, which doesn't allow the child or loved one the freedom to explore the world and gain confidence mastering life's skills, e.g. parent who rushes in and tells her children what to do without really listening to their feelings sends this message: You can't take care of yourself or know your own feelings so I have to do all that for you.

Table 4.6

PERSONALITY TRAITS CORRESPONDING TO ATTACHMENT STYLES

Secure Attachment Style
Child feels secure, loved, lovable, and self confident

Ambivalent Attachment Style
Child is ambivalent, alternately angry and clinging, showing a basic distrust of self. "I must avoid Mum's anger by avoiding acknowledgment of my own difficult feelings, pushing them down, switching them off."

Avoidant Attachment Style
Child is avoidant, watchful, wary, showing a basic distrust of others.
"Sometimes Mum's OK, sometimes not. I must watch carefully and modify my mood and feelings to hers (some of these children become distant and avoid others, some become anxious and clingy in their efforts to solve dilemmas.)

Disorganized Attachment Style
Child is angry and clingy (distrusting self); others are not trustworthy (distrusting others), but abusive and I deserve it. "Mum is so unpredictable I just don't know what to do for the best, I'm afraid all the time."

Table 4.7

POTENTIAL FOR SHAME

An unmet need is a shamed need—unmet can mean the need is ignored (covert shaming), laughed at, criticized, mocked, made fun of, not taken seriously, talked about inappropriately, etc.

Borrowed *(existential)*

Community—location (right side of tracks, Bible belt, rural / urban); ethnicity (race, employment, religious), etc.

Family—employment, education, scandal, chronic illness, handicap, religion, child unwanted

Personal

The following parts may be shamed by ridicule, teasing, disrespecting privacy, belittling, forbidding, disapproving, punishing, mocking, no role modeling, no guidance on handling, no preparation for development, withdrawing or taking personal offense when developmental needs expressed

Body—parts; functions; movements

Emotions—excitement / joy; hope; quiet; anxiety; anger; sadness; fear; embarrassment; hurt

Drives—sexual, hunger

Interpersonal needs—Empathy; companionship; touching, holding, hugging; to differentiate (be different)/ to identify; affirmation; power / competency; help; acceptance

Intellectual—IQ; too bookish / not bookish enough; think too much / not enough; stink at math / language…; illogical; memory

Image—Flawless / totally flawed; competent / incompetent; peace maker / trouble maker; in control; clone-like; self-sufficient / helpless

Spiritual—beliefs / lack of beliefs; practice of beliefs

Purpose—gifts / ability to contribute to society; God's plan reflects individuality

Chapter 5

Defending Against Shame

"I do not understand what I do.
For what I want to do I do not do, but what I hate I do".

Romans 7: 15

*I*n the movie, "The Secret Life of Bees" taken from the book by Sue Monk Kidd[1], we cringe in the opening scene. An altercation is taking place between a husband and wife while their daughter watches. The mother is packing her suitcase when the father begins using physical force to keep her from leaving. In their struggle, a gun falls to the floor. Their four-year-old daughter picks up the weapon, it discharges, and kills the mother instantly. We then watch this little girl survive her father's physical abuse that continues throughout her childhood until she is a teenager and runs away with her nanny. They find respite in a safe haven. Not only is it a place of safety, but she learns the truth about her mother's intentions that fateful night. Eventually her violent father tracks and finds them. With love winning out, he decides to leave her in this safe place. Her final question to her father concerned the lie that he told her all of her growing up years: that her mother was leaving the two of them. "Why," she pleads with him "…didn't you tell me she was taking me with her?" His one sentence explanation was, "Because she wasn't taking *me* with her." And so we realize that the rage that characterized her father's personality and his way of relating to his daughter was protecting him from shame – the shame of being left by his wife.

Understanding the soul-wrenching depth of pain brought on by shame is crucial to imagining the unacceptable behaviors our psychological mechanisms resort to in an effort to avoid such pain. Understanding that pain, the deep hurt of losing our worth as a human being, as described in chapter one, helps us to understand the unreasonable and self-defeating behaviors we unwittingly employ to protect us from shame. In other words, before realizing that shame is involved, we will do most anything to avoid that kind of pain. And it is our avoiding behaviors that have the effect of shaming our offspring and assaulting our relationships. So one benefit of this book is to bring our shame into our awareness. What follows is a discussion of many of those behaviors that can solidify into personality traits.

Before looking at a list of some major avoidance patterns, let us consider a category unto itself – addiction. Minirth, Meier, and Arterburn write "…shame is the issue that drives almost every compulsive, self-defeating behavior known to the human race. Shame is at the root of all addictions[2]. In the world of substance abuse, those bravely recovering from their addictions learn that shame played a huge role in maintaining their addiction. The drug of choice anesthetizes the pain of feeling worthless. But the escape from the pain of lost worth is short-lived. The addictive cycle inevitably takes the user into the pit of shame when the high or the rush is over. And the pain of the shame for using their drug of choice, their escaping behaviors, tempts addicts to escape once again to that drug of choice. The same cycle is recognized by those whose addiction is about sexually acting out, or over eating, or shopping, or whatever compulsive pattern has become an anesthetic to numb out the pain of shame.

In addition to addictions, we will look at other patterns we may have developed to avoid shame. Table 5.1, *Defending Against Shame*[3] is not an exhaustive list. Not only does it not include the addictive cycle, described above, it does not list compulsive patterns such as excessive television viewing and compulsively playing games of a technological nature. So as we focus on these particular avoidance behaviors, let us keep an open mind in order to recognize our own tendencies for avoiding a shame attack.

Notice that the first defense listed is *rage*. When we are intensely angry, we are very focused on the cause of our anger. Rage carries the element of revenge. We want to punish and shame the offender. All the angry thoughts, the angry energy, and shame is being directed onto something beyond ourselves. Rage consumes us. We simply do not have the capacity to experience shame welling up within while we are raging. All of our emotional capacity is consumed in this experience. So it works. The rage keeps the shame from being released. We are successfully avoiding a shame attack.

The next defense listed is *contempt.* The business of contempt is to elevate ourselves above others by shaming them, while remaining calm, cool, and collected. We are, in effect, sending them down into the pit of shame in lieu of our own plunge into that pit, or we are projecting our shame onto them. Again, it works.

The next defense, *striving for perfection,* can be particularly problematic in devoutly religious communities. To defend against constant threats of feeling inadequate or inherently defective, or unspiritual, we can get caught up in perfectionism, especially when certain Biblical verses, misunderstood or taken out of context, seem to call us to perform perfectly. In fact perfectionism is blatantly legalistic. It focuses on standards or laws that are of human construction. And scripture declares repeatedly that to rely on living up to standards is to abandon God's grace.

> *"All who rely on observing the law are under a curse..." Galatians 3:10*

The verse found in the sermon on the mount is particularly misunderstood.

> *" Be perfect, therefore, as your heavenly Father is perfect." Matthew 6:48*

104

The exegesis of the above verses by Albers and Clements[4] reflects the context of love for the above verse – what the "therefore" is about. The verse speaks to an "...encouragement toward wholeness and growth in relationships... [and] those who would profess to be perfect or sinless are deceiving and lying to themselves."

> "*...speaking the truth in love, we will in all things grow up into Him who is the Head, that is, Christ.*" *Ephesians 4:15*

> "*But grow in the grace and knowledge of our Lord and Savior Jesus Christ...*" *2 Peter 3:18*

> "*If we claim to be without sin, we deceive ourselves, and the truth is not in us.*" *1 John 1:8*

Performing perfectly is a self-centered focus on works that suggests we can become more acceptable to God. Whereas scripture calls us to a very different mind-set.

> "*Keep your behavior excellent among the Gentiles, so that in the thing in which they slander you as evil-doers, they may because of your good deeds, as they observe them, glorify God in the day of visitation.*" *1 Peter 2:12 (New American Standard Bible)*

Because this is a prevalent defense, we will look at it in detail in Table 5.2, *Perfection – The Enemy of Excellence*[5]. Turn now and examine the contrast of perfection and excellence.

Perfectionism is contrasted with the Biblical admonition of pursuing excellence. The *outlook* for perfectionism is idealistic and not at all realistic. Notions of how things "should be" crowd out a realistic perspective. It is very challenging for a perfectionist to accept something undesirable as "it is what it is". (We will be looking specifically at our own compilation of those inhumane ideals of how things "should be" in chapter 9.) The perfectionist *strives for* the impossible in a demand for the perfect, while the pursuit of excellence helps us accept the possible. Continuing with Table 5.2, notice how the *self-talk* of the perfectionist can be extremely oppressive. These demands seem to come from an external authority, carrying this unverbalized consequence: If I don't satisfy these demands, shame on me. The family that promotes perfectionism, imposes a requirement to comply with a perfect image, usually vaguely defined, and if we attain it, they will "up" the ante. If you get those "Cs" up to "Bs", the next requirement will be "As". The bottom line of this dynamic is that anything less than perfect is shameful.

Continuing with Table 5.2, the perfectionist's *motivation* is avoiding the shame of failure, while the pursuer of excellence is focused on the positive to be gained with success. The *product* is the focus in perfectionism versus the *process* being the focus in the pursuit of excellence. The difference in motivation explains why the perfectionist rarely can celebrate a completed stage of a project. The end result is all that matters. Whereas the pursuer of excellence can appreciate little successes along the way. Think about which person you want on your committee. Which one has the better opportunity to enjoy the journey?

At this point we can see that the *position is* enslaving for perfectionism. There is no freedom to accept that a flaw does not need to ruin an endeavor. By definition excellence is not annihilated by a flaw. Notice the *view of life* described as a dreaded curse versus a challenge that is welcomed. Considering these characteristics of perfectionism helps us to understand the use of the word "curse" in Gal. 3:10, as noted above. The contrast of perfectionism with the pursuit of excellence reveals very different fruit (results) from each mind-set. As you finish reading Table 5.2, can you sense the more relaxed, easy-going, relational way embedded in the pursuit of excellence?

Striving for power is the next defense listed. Sometimes this is exhibited in people rather obviously, such as jockeying for the top position in a social setting. They keep the limelight on themselves by following a story with one that tops the previous one, using a take control comment such as, "You think that's something, wait till you hear this one." Others may strive for power to adhere to their internalized ideals, risking becoming self-righteous. In a similar vein some of us count on our personal power (will power) to control our compulsive behaviors, refusing to access help such as that of a support group. Another power trip can be seen in an attempt to be everything another person needs – to make another happy or rescue one who is struggling with misfortunes. Other power plays show up in one who assumes undue authority, or undue wisdom. When an extremely authoritative or wise image is established, others tend to keep their opinions and ideas at a minimum. So this leaves the powerful one at little risk for exposure of a flaw that might trigger a shame attack. If that power-filled demeanor conveys that one has it all together, can never be wrong, many people will be reluctant to question or differ from the powerful one. And so the growth-producing experiences of iron sharpening iron are unlikely to happen.

"As iron sharpens iron, so one man sharpens another."

Proverbs 27:17

Coming across as the font of wisdom and authority to avoid a shame attack, results in stymied growth.

Blame is the next defense listed. If we are busy blaming self or another for a mishap, we will probably succeed at avoiding shame. Now one might wonder how does blaming yourself work? It seems that would bring on the shame. The shame experienced by self-blame may be less than the shame of being blamed by another. So if beating up yourself beats the other person to it, the other may lessen the amount of shame extended in the situation. Blaming can work several different ways. If the blaming is launched with a lot of anger, then the same mechanism as that of rage would be in effect. Angry blaming can be emotionally consuming. Blaming another may also be a way of projecting one's own shame onto the other. And finally, blaming can come from a desire to regain control after or during a mishap. An illusion of control is created by the implication that since we can apply blame, we appear to completely understand what went wrong so that the mishap will never happen again. And so the myth of no more mishaps is perpetuated, reinforcing a false sense of having no vulnerability for a shame attack.

The next defense against shame is among the less obvious. *Internal withdrawal* deserves our undivided attention. I refer to this way of avoiding shame as the favorite defense of the primary member of the "nice-nice" family. And they live next door to the "looking good" family. These folks do not have any shame. They have it all tucked away. Internal withdrawal refers to a removal of the real self to reduce the risk of exposure of an unacceptable part that might trigger a shame attack. The real self is pulled back into a private world, back stage, and there is a public self that comes forward and takes center stage. The real self with its needs, it's feelings (including shame), its imaginations, even sometimes its dreams and aspirations, is all gathered together and pulled back behind closed doors, with shades pulled down, hiding under the covers. The real self is hidden to protect it from any exposure, avoiding a shame attack. When presenting this material in workshops, I emphasize the defense of internal withdrawal with a tee shirt. As I hold it up for all to see, I comment "The lights are on" and then they read on the shirt, "No One Home". As facial expressions of "I get it" sweep across the room, I turn the shirt to the other side where they read "Place feet here." And this highlights the sad reality that when internal withdrawal prevails, we are at a huge risk for becoming doormats. If our emotions of hurt, sadness, fear, shame, and anger are not allowed, we are not teaching others who we are according to what is going on inside of us. So people tend to offend, take advantage, use, and abuse us partially because they do not know us and specifically because we do not push back (meaning to speak up), presenting them with negative consequences and giving them an opportunity to know the real us. We do not speak up and thus present them with a false sense of who we are. So in the name of being a nice person or a good Christian we create a facade. This invulnerable public self reduces the risks of shame attacks. But it costs us dearly in terms of rich and intimate relationships. As one author explains, "If we deny or cover up anything that is at home in the soul, then we cannot be fully present to others. Hiding the dark places results in a loss of soul; speaking for and from them offers a way toward genuine community and intimacy."[6]

The next defense may be a complete surprise. It is *humor*. At this point, some will be thinking, "Oh no, nothing is exempt." And that is the truth. We are so ingenious, we can use anything to avoid feeling shame, humor included. God gave us a wonderful gift when He gave us humor. Perhaps you have read the latest medical literature about laughter and its positive effect on our chemistry. Of course the effect of a good laugh is Biblically described as good medicine.

"A cheerful heart is good medicine..." Proverbs 17:22

However like anything else, humor can be abused by using it to distance people. And why might we need to distance people? By now you will be able to guess. We are keeping ourselves safe from something shameful being seen in us. Another abuse of humor is to use it to hide mocking thoughts we are having toward another. We avoid blatantly shaming others when we cloak our mocking attitude in humor. Other variations on this theme include a combination of humor with contempt that produces cynicism or sarcasm. So the question becomes one of whether I am flexible, freely choosing humor and noticing if the other person is thoroughly enjoying the humor, versus using it to control the conversation and avoid anything showing up that is shameful about me.

The last avoidance pattern listed is *denial*. Some of us have experienced enough shame about our feelings, our needs, our desires that they have been repressed out of our awareness. We attempt to manage life as if God had omitted these parts from our finiteness. One way we maintain denial about feelings, and shame in particular, is by being task-centered, practical-type people. We are going to get the job done. Feelings about the job or anything related to the task have no relevance, no validity. We measure success by whether we got the job done. But we do not know one another. The depth of our relationships is limited by ignoring our own feelings or those of another. When we have pretended we have no feelings, needs, or desires over a period of time, they get repressed and are not available to us. Therefore our denial keeps our emotional alarm system from warning us that we are being disrespected. We are handicapped by having no awareness that something is wrong with this picture. Likewise our positive emotions cannot be fully experienced and shared because they have been caught up in the repression process too. Our internal radar is malfunctioning. However, despite our denial, when we are shamed, the shame slips in under the radar and is given secret storage. Keeping that shame stored in its secret place to avoid a shame attack requires significant emotional energy. And so the public self must take center stage, though emotional energy is being depleted, and the real self must stay unavailable. It is an exhausting way to do life.

This chapter's listing of defenses against experiencing a shame attack can help us begin to estimate the extent of shame we harbor by noting how much we use our defenses. Though we may be defensive for other reasons, avoiding shame headlines the possibilities. Therefore it can be profitable to notice the situations in which we employ our pattern of defensiveness – a red flag that we may be vulnerable for a shame attack. And our vulnerability can be a clue to some part of us that has shame wrapped around it. It is like working backwards to discover shame. For example, Rosemary became curious about her use of contempt to manage her own shame. She recognized that frequently she criticized other women for the way they groomed themselves, how they applied makeup in particular.

As she considered the list of defenses, she reluctantly owned that she becomes contemptuous in her criticism. Her introspective journey led her to remember how she had been ridiculed when she was a pre-teen for trying out her mother's makeup. Her memory made her wince as she could still hear her father's mocking words accusing her of "… trying to act like a woman and ending up looking like a slut." So her desire to be attractive, to enjoy her femininity reaped her so much pain, in that shaming encounter with her father, that she repressed that desire. In other words, shame was wrapped around her inclination to enjoy her femininity and that inclination was ushered out of her awareness.

Another example of using our defenses to avoid shame is about a man called Ralph. The moment he recounted in therapy was, at first glance, a trivial one. Yet he pursued it to learn more about his defensive reactions. His neighbor walked over to Ralph's driveway to admire Ralph's new car. So as the neighbor compliments Ralph, "nice looking wheels", Ralph attempts to make a joke about his old car. As he focused on the possibility of that attempt at humor and his deflection of the compliment being a defense against shame, he recalled his own father's boastfulness about finding good used cars. His father had so self-assuredly emphasized how this was the smart thing to do that Ralph experienced the unverbalized agenda of shame on you if you do not do it my way. As is frequently the result of an extreme emphasis on the one right way, the hidden consequence is shame on you if you choose any other way.

Just as a coin has two sides, defensive actions can be negative and positive. We have looked at some of the major ways of defending that are negative. They have ranged from passive, giving up the real self to appear to be a "nice" person, to destructively acting out. But the other side of this coin is about positively impacting one's world. People can also be avoiding shame by pursuing success in very socially acceptable behaviors. Lewis Smedes[7] writes of one illustrative example. This very bright little boy was born to a couple that totally pursued their own ambitions and pleasures, leaving all the care of their son to a nanny. Even in failure, as the father's career in English parliament crashed, the boy was not brought to the forefront of their attention. From boarding school he pleaded with mother and father to visit him, to no avail. Fortunately the nanny, the only one home during the boarding school's holiday breaks, tried to be there for him. But she could not adequately fill the shoes of needed parents. The boy grows up convinced that he was not worth loving, but began to cope with that belief by achieving. His nanny remained supportive, and he thrust himself into honor and glory. This man was Winston Churchill — who, as an adult, earned great respect from much of the world.

As we close this chapter on some of the defenses used to manage shame, I encourage each of us to look for our own behaviors in this discussion. Or we may add to this list other behaviors that annoy or distance those we relate to or any behaviors that have a compulsive flavor to them. We have the opportunity then to work backwards as in the examples of Rosemary and Ralph. Shame is such a stealthy emotion! Therefore working backwards from our defensiveness to discover this emotion can be very helpful in the pursuit of the healing of shame.

Table 5.1

DEFENDING AGAINST SHAME (AVOIDING FEELING SHAME)

Rage	Transfer of blame
Contempt	Internal withdrawal
Striving for perfection	Humor
Striving for power	Denial

Table 5.2

	PERFECTION— THE ENEMY OF EXCELLENCE	
	Perfectionism	**Excellence**
Outlook	Idealistic: "It should be…"	Realistic: "It is…"
Striving For	The impossible—desires the perfect	The possible—accepts the possible
Self-talk	I must… I should… I ought to… I have to…	I want… I wish… I would like… I'm attempting…
Stated as	Always a demand	A request or desire
Motivation	Avoidance of negative Fear of failure	Striving for positive Desire for success
Focus on	Product	Process
Position is	Slave…in prison of perfectionism	Free…in pursuit of excellence
Expects	Best in comparison to everyone else	Best of self
Life Viewed as	Curse that is dreaded	Challenge that is welcomed
Results	Disappointment Condemnation Frustration Failure	Accomplishment Acceptance Fulfillment Success
Live in	Fantasy Unreal world	Reality Real world
Bottom line	A lie: People and things do have the ability to be perfect	The truth: People and things do NOT have the ability to be perfect.

Chapter 6

Shame and Integrity

*H*opefully the earlier chapters of this book helped each of us to become aware of some of the parts that have been shamed. In the exercise in this chapter we will choose a shamed part and verbally take it back into who we are. Ideally we would engage a safe person to participate in this exercise with us. Books are devoted to helping us discern a safe person from a non-safe person.[1] Briefly, let us consider safe people as those who experience the tender, forgiving grace of God consistently in their own lives. And out of that relationship with God they are most likely to be non-judgmental, caring, accepting, naturally extending the grace they know to others. They also appreciate confidentiality, knowing this is our story to tell as we choose. On the other hand, an unsafe person might be recognized when we are "…being manipulated with condemnation whenever the other person suggests that you need to be more, better, or different than you are." And so safe people appreciate our steps toward wholeness. They would be honored to participate in this exercise because they would be involved in our transformation.

An illustration of owning a sinful capacity comes from a workshop I was presenting to the leadership of a church. The leadership of the church's Celebrate Recovery program was pursuing training in the area of domestic violence, because their ministry was encountering families struggling with violence in their homes. As I addressed those who would be ministering to the perpetrators of violence, I issued a stern warning. "If you are unable to own that the capacity to be violent toward a family member exists within you, I urge you to consider that you are not ready to minister to these folks." I then made a reference to the scene of the Pharisee and the sinner praying in the temple. Remember that the Pharisee totally disowned even the capacity to sin.

Let us be encouraged that when a part of our sinful nature or our finite nature is integrated into our awareness, then, and only then, can it be submitted to the Lordship of Jesus Christ. As we humbly own the previously denied parts of who we are, God can do with it as He pleases. And this is the work of His transforming grace. Note the following verse now as well as midway and at the close of this chapter.

"And we…are being transformed into his likeness with every-increasing glory, which comes from the Lord, who is the Spirit." 2 Corinthians 3:18

So a part of us gets wrapped in shame (sometimes several layers) and because of the painful layers of shame wrapped around that part, we push that part out of our awareness. Or we develop escapes into anesthetizing or distracting behaviors.

Now the imagery of layers is a useful way of thinking about degree of shame – how much shame we have around a part of something about us. Generally speaking the number of layers of shame correspond to how unaware we are of the part. Or the number of layers correspond to the compulsiveness and destructiveness of the behaviors that create our escape. Also the number of layers correspond to how much our sense of worth is impacted when that part is exposed. We will now look at a concept called integrity. You will notice that the concept differs somewhat from the usual definition of integrity.

Let us start at the beginning when a part of us gets shamed. The backdrop is that for us as children, the significant adults in our life are always right. Even if a child protests certain treatment, i.e. complaining or tattling to another adult, the child is internalizing subconsciously that the adult is doing what is right. Therefore, the child assumes the ultimate blame for the pain experienced. And specifically the part of the child that is involved in the shaming gets blamed.

Theorists postulate that a child's need for security requires that the child assume the blame. For a child to perceive the adult as being inappropriate would introduce too much danger and insecurity into the child's world.

So the child experiences the adult as right and assumes that the pain is deserved due to a faulty part, an unacceptable part, or a blameworthy part of the child. This designated part seems to cause the pain. For example, a child's perceptions might form like this: If it were not for my unruly hair, I would not be made fun of – my unruly hair is the cause of my getting made fun of –my unruly hair is the cause of my getting shamed. The next logical place for this child to go with that assumption is, "My unruly hair is shameful."

So the need, the feeling, whatever was getting shamed, seems to be the cause of the shame. "Since the painful shaming is about my unruly hair–my unruly hair is shameful." Though this type of shamed part is difficult to hide, this child may wear a hat most of the time, and probably will not mention his unruly hair. That is the best he can do to disown this shamed part. But what about features that are not physical and therefore easier to hide?

A little girl who gets a new dress is twirling around in her God-given delight and expressing her God-given need for affirmation from the important adults in her life. She either gets the needed affirmation or she gets shamed. Remember an unmet need is a shamed need.

So the seemingly benign response she may experience of "umm…" uttered from behind a newspaper does not meet the need and actually shames her attempt to get affirmation, which ultimately shames her *need* for affirmation. If she experiences sufficient shame when this need (to have her femininity affirmed, admired, by delighted adults) shows up, she is likely to disown this need. In her perspective, exhibiting the need reaps her too much pain. It is not worth it.

The disowning of the need is an effort to see to it that this painful shaming experience is not repeated. "If I simply stop needing the affirmation, the adults to delight in admiring me, then I will not seek it, sparing myself being wounded once again by the shaming response." A typical symptom of shame around this need would be this girl growing up and choosing to dress in a dowdy or unflattering way.

The blamed part is getting shame wrapped around it and ushered out of her awareness to her subconscious as she adopts a pretense of not having the need. It is relegated to the unknown part of her identity, probably to be triggered someday when her daughter displays that same need. Perhaps the daughter would begin to experiment with make-up. Almost like a reflex, the mother may shame her daughter. She may forbid the experimenting with tones of disgust that convey "shame on you". Then her daughter is likely to carry the family tradition of shame on that need. Or she may experience shame in the opposite direction, shame for her mother's shame. And, if so, her coping behavior may be opposite that of her mother's coping ways. She could become so focused on wearing makeup that she over indulges, seeming to be obsessed with grooming. Either way, the shame is passed on to the next generation.

Let us consider one more example of this split-off part dynamic. A little boy approaches his dad and says, "Look at my muscle," as he flexes his bicep with all his might. The kind of response he gets determines shame or worth and value regarding his masculinity. If the response is apathetic or mocking, his need to have his masculinity affirmed gets shamed. Later his attempt to keep that shame buried may prompt him to shame any physique that is not muscle bound, as he becomes obsessed with body building. So he gets stuck trying to avoid shame by building an extraordinary physique and will never be satisfied. What he is trying to accomplish is more about managing that shame than it is about muscle strength.

Thus we arrive into adulthood fragmented. We have split-off parts of our identity. In essence we have a broken heart. And it is this fragmented self, with missing parts, that constitutes our public self. The real self includes the totality of who we are. The public self differs from the real self to the extent that parts of us have been split off and disowned. The more the real self and public self differ, the more relationships suffer. They are robbed of intimacy because the whole person is not available to be known, but parts are hidden deeply to avoid pain. The distancing that takes place in our earthly relationships pales in comparison to the distance between God and us. We are drawn to God and we surrender ourselves to Him. However all we are able to surrender is that which we know. Though

He welcomes all we bring to Him, our unawareness of those missing parts limits the extent of our surrender. He draws us toward an intimate relationship with Himself to heal our broken hearts. He wants to increase our capacity for intimacy. He wants to make us whole.

"He heals the brokenhearted and binds up their wounds." Psalm 147:3

A significant part of the healing process is the reclaiming of the split-off or hidden parts. As those parts are owned, are acknowledged as belonging to our identity, they can then be surrendered to God so that the Holy Spirit can hold sway over them. In other words, refusing to own certain aspects of who we are keeps the Holy Spirit from accessing those parts and impedes God's sanctifying grace. Owning these layered-in-shame parts sets the scene for God's agenda of transformation.

"And we, who with unveiled faces all reflect the Lord's glory, are being transformed into his likeness with ever-increasing glory, which comes from the Lord, who is the Spirit." 2 Corinthians 3:18

Table 6.1 gives us a graphic illustration of a heart that is broken with parts missing. Also this table depicts some of the aspects of our finite nature. Notice in particular the first items listed under finite nature. They are likely to be the categories of our disowned parts. In fact many of these aspects are treated as if they are sinful. Again I refer to anger as an example of a disowned part. Of course scripture can clarify the confusion about this much maligned emotion.

> *"Be angry but do not sin;" Ephesians 4:26 (The Revised Standard Version)*

Even those parts that are in fact sinful by Biblical description need to be received back into our awareness, back into our identity. As with the foibles of our finite nature, the capacities rooted in our sinful nature need to be owned also. We are needing to own our capacities for revenge, jealousy, lust, idolatry, gossip, meanness, rebellion, self-absorption, insensitivity, rudeness,—a never ending list. Likewise we are subject to the entire range of the human condition such as being unspiritual, petty, unloving, lonely, manipulative, needy, demanding attention/praise/encouragement – another never ending list. One expert parallels the descriptions of the outcasts of Jesus' society as being descriptions about the outcasts, the unlovable, the impure, the abandoned –the shamed—*in* all of us, not just *outside* of us."[2] When we resist owning these parts of who we are, we are in serious danger of joining the Pharisee in the temple that Jesus described as confident in his own righteousness. We are constantly in danger of declaring ourselves to be the exceptional human being.

> *"The Pharisee stood up and prayed about himself: 'God, I thank you that I am not like all other*

men—robbers, evildoers, adulterers—or even like the tax collector'." Luke 18:11

Notice that the proud Pharisee is not boasting about not having committed those particular sins. He is ruling out any *capacity* for sin as he places himself above other men.

The sinful choices that spring from our sinful nature must be acknowledged and responded to appropriately. Details about that appropriate response will follow in chapter 10. So our shamed parts and our sinful capacities must be received into our identity.

Following is an exercise designed to walk us into the experience of reclaiming the parts we have deemed unacceptable. Lest we become anxious about welcoming unacceptable parts back into our identity, let us remember that the cause is a Godly one. We are cooperating with God's desire to heal our broken hearts. We are expressing our desire for that healing. And we are positioning these shamed parts so that they can be managed by the Holy Spirit.

An example of this "Reclaiming Exercise" is one shared by Dr. Curtis A. Levang, in a presentation at a conference of Christian Association of Psychological Studies.[3] He described a man who suffered as a child with a chronic ear infection. And the nature of his particular infection required a topical medicine that had a distinctive foul odor. Now you can imagine the rest of the story, knowing what children tend to do. His classmates dubbed him "Stinky Ears."

So to do this reclaiming exercise this man needed to say "Stinky Ears, you are me, I can accept you. I take you back into who I am." Regarding this particular issue, if a witness, a safe person, is available, the witness would repeat the reclamation by saying, "You are saying stinky ears is a part of you."

Sometimes we do not have a name or a label like that. It may be simply descriptive such as:

* "little girl who needed her dad's admiration".
* "little boy who was a klutz in sports"
* "little girl who was not as pretty as her sister"
* "little boy who was a pest"
* "little girl who kept her mother from a career"
* "little boy who could never measure up to his dad"
* "little girl who was a sexual toy for others

Consider my disallowed anger described earlier as an example. In the practice of reclaiming, I would say, "Little girl whose anger was dangerous and unacceptable, I accept your anger. I take anger back into who I am." And the witness would say, "You are saying anger is a part of you." The response of the witness helps to seal the transaction.

It is hoped these examples can bring to mind a shame-filled experience. This exercise calls for us to step into the discomfort of owning those shameful parts, or in some cases, welcoming back that shame-filled child. Again a safe person to participate in this with you is ideal. Someone acting as a witness makes the effort more real. Be warned that this exercise can create discomfort. By definition, as we focus on a shamed part or shaming experience, we are stepping into pain.

In the healing process described in subsequent chapters, we will be looking at how we put ourselves into a healing posture. Reclaiming makes a significant contribution to the process of putting ourselves in that healing posture. So I encourage the practice of reclaiming. Consider who would qualify as a safe person for you and make an appointment to practice this reclaiming exercise. Or stop reading here and now and practice taking back a shamed part of you, speaking aloud. Then when it is recommended as a part of the healing process later in the book, your familiarity with *reclaiming* will help you apply it. So as we integrate the shamed, missing parts back into our identity, we are strengthening our integrity. When less of each of us is outcast, we are far more able to know that but by the grace of God there go I. When what has been outcast is taken back in, we can relate to others' confessions with a stronger capacity for empathy. As our integrity grows, our tendency to be judgmental shrinks.

Let us be encouraged that when a part of our sinful nature or our finite nature is integrated into our awareness, then, and only then, can it be submitted to the Lordship of Jesus Christ. As we humbly own previously denied parts of who we are, God can do with it as He pleases. And this is the work of His transforming grace. This chapter closes with that verse about this transformation.

"And we...are being transformed into his likeness with every-increasing glory, which comes from the Lord, who is the Spirit." 2 Corinthians 3:18

Table 6.1

INTEGRITY VS. FRAGMENTATION

"If we say we have no sin, we deceive ourselves, and the truth is not in us."
I John 1:8

"The Pharisee stood and prayed thus with himself, 'God, I thank thee that I am not like other men'..." Luke 18:11

Sinful / Finite Nature

Imperfect	Acceptable
Foibles	Creative
Needs	Gifted
Feelings	Valuable
Drives	Intentional
Insecure	Useful
Flawed	Glorifying
Worthy	Friend
Loved / lovable	Loving
Holy	

"The Spirit of the Lord God is upon me, because the LORD has anointed me to bring good tidings to the afflicted; he has sent me to bind up the brokenhearted, to proclaim liberty to the captives, and the opening of the prison to those who are bound...to comfort all who mourn; to grant...a garland instead of ashes, the oil of gladness instead of mourning, the mantle of praise instead of a faint spirit; that they may be called oaks of righteousness, the planting of the LORD, that he may be glorified. They shall build up the ancient ruins, they shall raise up the former devastation; they shall repair the ruined cities, the devastations of many generations." Isaiah 61:1-4

Chapter 7

Shame and Your Gifts

"When I stand before God at the end of my life, I would hope that I would not have a single bit of talent left and be able to say, 'I used everything You gave me'." [1] Erma Bombeck

young woman that I had the privilege of working with kindly offered to write a part of her story for this chapter of the book. I gratefully share it with admiration for her.

"Being a child of divorce is never easy, nor is it easy to raise children in a divorce-remarriage situation. But, like any young girl, I loved my dad, and very much wanted my stepmother to like me. She didn't have much experience with kids, and was nervous around my sister and me. My stepmother also had a beautiful voice, and she would often sing in the car when we were with her. I always admired how lovely it sounded. Sometimes, when just my dad picked me up for weekend visits, he and I would sing along to the radio—jokingly, usually, but special. Just the two of us.

My stepmother also liked to have her house neat, so when I spent weekends with them, Saturday mornings were chore time. This particular Saturday—sometime when I was about 11—I was cleaning my room, and as usual, was performing what was certainly an epic concert. My Pointer Sisters record was spinning, the hairbrush a perfect microphone to allow me to reach the millions of adoring fans on the other side of the mirror. As I bopped around the room, I paid little attention to the actual cleaning at hand. But, at some point, I needed something in the kitchen—a cleaning supply, a glass of water, I don't precisely recall what. As I neared the kitchen, I overheard my stepmother talking to someone on the phone. She was talking about me—"Jennifer actually thinks she can sing." And a laugh.

I was mortified. I spun and flew back to my room, the hot blush crawling from my neck all the way to the roots of my hair. I turned the record off, put the hairbrush back, and vowed that I would never let anyone hear me sing again.

And I didn't. I briefly took a choir class in middle school, but sang under my breath until I convinced my mother to let me switch to another elective. No more slumber party concerts, no singing in church, no humming along to the radio—unless—unless I was convinced no one could hear me. Because I love to sing. Love it more than just about anything. It always makes me happy to cut loose—when no one is around—and imagine jaws dropping at the melodies pouring out of me.

My high school boyfriend, who would eventually become my husband, could melt a room with his voice. He sang in bands, competed in music competitions, played multiple instruments, and generally surrounded himself with music. On long road trips or casual Sunday mornings together, he would beg me to sing with him—just for fun. He promised that he wouldn't care if I was bad. But I couldn't do it, no matter how much it would have meant to him. Copious amounts of alcohol were necessary to persuade me to join a group of people for karaoke—and even in that intoxicated state, I still know enough to stand far back from the microphone and let others carry the performance.

I just couldn't shake the deep feeling of shame produced by being mocked as a child! Over the years I had become convinced that my lack of singing ability was a character flaw. I was certain that something was wrong with me, because I was such a horrible singer. Most people can at least carry a tune, I thought, or else they aren't bothered if they are a little off- key. But I couldn't sing a note AND I couldn't just be ok with letting my tone-deaf flag fly! I was obviously a deeply flawed person.

Twenty years after hearing my stepmother make fun of me, my beloved husband died after a 15- month battle with cancer. The year following his death was beyond crippling, a yawning chasm of pain, misery, aching loneliness, confusion, and despair. After stumbling through the first year, lost in a fog of grief, I faced the next year with the conviction that I was going to have to find something that would make me happy. One, simple something that could brighten my days and provide at least a brief respite from the physical labor of grieving. Singing. Of course.

I had sat by my husband's bed side and watched him take his last breath. Suddenly I realized that nothing could scare me as much as that moment had. So what if someone heard me sing off key? That person had no idea what I had seen, no idea what I had survived. I decided that life is too short to be scared, to be crippled by other peoples' opinions of me. I was beginning the process of becoming a new person without my husband, and frankly, that person wants to sing. So I signed up for singing lessons, focused on taking down the fears and insecurities that plagued me, one at a time.

I would love to say that I burst into my first lesson, confident and brave, and out of my mouth poured a heaven-sent sound. Neither of those things happened. As I walked into the small room where I would take my private lesson, I realized the rooms weren't sound-proof. All sorts of people passing down the hall could hear me. More importantly, my voice instructor would hear me. And then I would have to see him *again*. Horrifying. My heart began to pound.

My instructor introduced himself and told me a little about his musical background. I immediately apologized for what he was going to have to endure. And told him that it was okay if he didn't want to teach me. And that he could cancel our sessions if he decided

I was hopeless. And that I was sorry. So, so, very sorry. I must have been shouting over top of my pounding heart. Puzzled, he politely asked me what I had prepared to sing today. I burst out laughing. That's hilarious, I told him—do you think I am just going to sing right in front of you? We hardly know each other!

After a somewhat awkward silence, my instructor asks me if I know the lyrics to any songs. Of course, I tell him. Great, he says— let's sing one of those. Silence. I have absolutely no intention of singing in front of him. My palms are sweating, my heart is racing. In my mind, I am seeing my 11-year-old self hear how horrible I am at singing. Not a chance that a peep comes out of my mouth, and I tell my instructor as much. He gently points out that singing is a large part of what one does at a voice lesson. Wisely, he dispenses with things like lyrics and words, and begins with simple scales, using nonsense sounds. I agree to try, watching him intently for any indication that my screeching is permanently damaging his ears.

Let's just be honest. It wasn't great. I was on-pitch occasionally, off-pitch quite a bit more. My instructor is endeavoring to understand why I am such a wreck. I share with him my secret childhood shame and the obvious character flaw of my tone-deafness. Undeterred, he tells me that voice is just an instrument. I wouldn't expect to pick up a clarinet and play it perfectly—why would I expect my voice to be any different?

Suddenly, all the shame drained out. It wasn't me. There wasn't anything wrong with me. I just didn't know how to do something—but

I could learn! More importantly, I was learning! I had signed up for lessons, showed up, squawked out some notes, and no one ran screaming from the room. I could do this. It didn't matter how good I was, or how much time it would take to get better. I had faced that fear, and stared it down. I faced that fear not because I had to, but because I chose to. Singing just made me happy, and I eliminated my shame— just for me."

Early in my practice of psychotherapy I began to discover that we deny much of the creativity inside us because it has been shamed and thus squelched. I felt sad and angry. Sad that God's design of creativity in each of us lay dormant and that He would not be glorified. Angry that the rich creative potential in many of us was not showing up to be an inspiring blessing to the rest of us. In this chapter I urge all of us to be open to possibilities. May we be willing to remember any creative urges that were buried long ago or at least shelved until a *better time*. Perhaps we are aware of creative ideas that are on hold, waiting for some influential person's approval, or time to devote to it, or more expertise to venture into it, or the resources to step into it. Or perhaps pursuing the unknown is too fraught with the possibility of failure. And failure is too fraught with shame. To fail or to be wrong is frequently layered with shame. One author describes the issue of being wrong as shameful this way. "…we have lived in systems that functioned on the 'right-wrong' justice scale. The person who was right was okay; the person who was wrong was shamed.

All value and worth may have depended on being right; to be wrong meant annihilation of self and self-esteem."[2]

When I am presenting this material in a seminar, two posters are on display with the following quotes:

"To live a creative life, we must lose our FEAR of being WRONG.[3] Joseph Chilton Pearce

" Be valiant in the attempt, yet not ashamed to fail." *Samuel Johnson*

I am in complete agreement with theologians that understand a part of being created in God's image is the creativity He designed within us. Therefore none of us is exempt from being creative. Now I use a broad concept of creativity. I believe that problem solving and synthesizing others' solutions and inventing devices and processes all come under the large umbrella of creativity. For example I felt creative the day that my car had three inches of ice over the wipers, the door lock frozen, and my first client of the day would soon be waiting at my office. I connected 3 extension cords to my hair dryer from the garage to the car, warmed the lock, thawed the blanket of ice over the wipers, and arrived at my office with no one waiting for a tardy therapist. I consider that problem solved creatively. And furthermore, I conceptualize that creativity as flowing from the same place the material for this book flows from or any artist's expression on canvas.

For some of us, our creativity is limited because we suffered some shaming criticism of our creative efforts in childhood. This is not to portray all criticism as shaming. Julia Cameron, author of The Artist's Way speaks to the difference.[4]

"...even the most severe criticism when it fairly hits the mark is apt to be greeted by an internal *Ah-hah!* If it shows the artist a new and valid path for work. The criticism that damages is that which disparages, dismisses, ridicules, or condemns. Shamed by such criticism, an artist may become blocked or stop sending work out into the world." She goes on to explain that, "In order to recover our sense of hope and the courage to create, we must acknowledge and mourn the scars that are blocking us."[5]

All children start experimenting with their creativity. Sometimes it is a crayoned mural on the wall. Whatever the attempts to be expressive may have been, they were primitive and raw. The budding talent was rough around the edges, maybe rough in the middle, too. Now the little creator is very vulnerable in those moments. If we felt approval and encouragement about our creativity, chances are we went on to develop it, expanding into other creative arenas. For that development or expansion to happen, we needed four types of encouragement:

1. ...the freedom for curiosity

2. ...the courage to explore
3. ...the courage to put something out for attention – "look at what I just did"
4. ...the freedom to make a mistake –the most important part of an environment where creativity is nurtured

We must be able to accept a creation that is less than perfect. And so a nurturing environment is void of shame when desires and dreams begin to be expressed. An example from my childhood comes to mind. I was nine years older than my little brother, George. One day when he was about three years old, my mother and I heard a crash and wailing coming from the kitchen. We went running to the rescue to find my little brother, with a dish towel hanging down his back, getting up off the floor. We soon determined that he suffered no serious bodily injury, but his heart was broken. Between the sobbing gasps for air, he managed to conclude, "Mama, I not no superman." So we understood his leap from the kitchen counter with his dish towel cape had been a failed experiment. To the best of my memory, our response was full of empathy, devoid of shame.

I am not suggesting that the creativity of little ones does not need guidance and limits. Sometimes the very survival of these little ones depends on such wisdom. But I am suggesting that parents need to develop the art form of protection of person and property without shaming the creativity.

At the end of this paragraph please consider stopping and giving yourself a chance to ponder your creativity. Identify a creative moment for you – yesterday, last week, last month. It doesn't matter when, just simply acknowledge something creative that came forth from you. Some people not only find this difficult to do, but may actually experience some shame around the effort to describe something they have done as creative. If this is so for you, take a couple of deep breaths. If acknowledging a creative moment or endeavor is difficult, I encourage you to share this with a safe person. Sharing our creativity is one of the ways God begins to heal the shame that covers our creativity, sometimes in multiple layers. However the person or group to share with should be wisely chosen. This is one of the principles in Table 7.1 *Developing Your Gifts* that follows on page 146.

Principles no. 1 and 2 is where some of us need to start. We have admired creative people and, yet, exempted ourselves from their creative world. Scripture is very clear that God endows us with certain gifts. In fact one of the strongest admonitions Jesus delivered during His ministry was to the servant in the parable who did not invest the talent entrusted to him. Recorded in Matthew 25 is the parable of the ten talents. It is a story of three men entrusted with some money to manage while their master went on a journey. When the master returns, he is pleased with two of his servants who doubled their holdings by investing. The third man allowed fear to rule his decisions and buried the talent entrusted to him. The strong admonition is against the servant for allowing his fear to keep him not only from taking a risk, but also from seeking to be so much in control, avoiding risk, that he refused a safe investment where it would at least earn interest. Our determination to avoid failure requires a zero tolerance of risk. You will see our tendencies to stay safe, to stay in control addressed in Table 7.1. **Principle no. 3** addresses the ultimate benefit when we risk using our talents. Notice the fear that is not of the Lord in **Principle no. 4.** The fear of being wrong, failing and experiencing shame reveals shallowness in our ability to trust God. By definition, entering into our creativity is a step into the unknown. And that step requires courage. "Courage is resistance to fear, mastery of fear, not absence of fear."[6] **Principle no. 5** addresses our demands for certainty because of our fear of the unknown. That fear of the unknown is addressed multiple times in scripture. One of my family's favorite verses is the one cited with Principle no. 5. The next **Principle, no. 6**, is about letting go of the illusions of perfectionism. (We have examined perfectionism in chapter 5.) In the beginning of a creative project, we usually need to run some rough ideas by somebody. The perfectionist finds this too risky. Before the project is shared with anyone, it needs to be final, set in stone in its perfection. And so needed help that comes with collaboration is forfeited. And frequently the result of this Lone Ranger approach is that the project is relegated to the mausoleum of undeveloped ideas. Consider the sadness evoked by this summation:

"Most of us go to our grave with our music still inside us."[7] Justice Oliver Wendell Holmes

Those illusions of perfectionism and certainty must be dealt a death blow if we are to become risk takers. Our determination to avoid appearing foolish, being a beginner, and failing must also be dealt a death blow. **Principle no. 7** challenges us to become willing to suffer in those ways. We deny that in order to do something well we must first be willing to do it badly. Instead, we opt for committing at the point where we feel assured of success. Basing what we will try on a promise of success may make us feel safe. But the cost of that safety may be feelings of being stifled, smothered, bored, ultimately at risk for despair. Safety based on certainty is a very expensive illusion. The nature of risk taking is summed up this way:

"There is the risk you cannot afford to take, there is the risk you cannot afford not to take."[8] Peter Drucker

As mentioned earlier, **Principle no. 8** is about where you share your creativity. The reality for some of us is that we have someone in our life who has a pattern of sometimes shaming us. It is not being judgmental to identify those who have exhibited that pattern. And, in fact, it is necessary to identify the danger of being shamed if we are to choose wisely when sharing the early stages of our creative endeavor. And then of course the final Principle is about choosing the safe person or a supportive environment for your creative effort. Especially in the early stages of a creative project, we need to find nurture and encouragement for our souls. You will notice the Biblical verse cited with each principle. Other scriptures may come to your mind that will motivate and inspire you. Some of us may remember shamed ambitions and dreams and need to grieve the inhibiting impact of that shame. If so, we also will need to forgive the offender for their insensitivity. Also, though you find support, much of creative endeavors require a significant amount of loneliness. I had not known before starting to convert this material from the seminar presentation to this book, just how lonely the work would leave me feeling. I have been richly blessed with encouragement from a variety of people. I would never have ventured in this direction without their encouragement. A wonderful example is my cousin, who stepped into the process offering her editing skills. However, despite the support, encouragement and involvement of others, I am keenly aware of no one working with me while I am doing the research or sitting at my computer. Even when I create a reward for my efforts by scheduling lunch with a friend, I am enduring the loneliness the other hours of the day.

So what might be some of those first steps into our creativity? Some paths may call for reading a book, taking a class, joining relevant groups, taking private lessons, or responding to particular requests by others. Our creative endeavor does not have to be in the scope of painting the Sistine Chapel. When we begin to respect our creativity by stepping into it, the Designer of that creativity is glorified. And to God be the glory!

I close this chapter with An Artist's Prayer:[9]

O Great Creator,

We are gathered together in your name

That we may be of greater service to you

And to our fellows.

We offer ourselves to you as instruments.

We open ourselves to your creativity in our lives.

We surrender to you our old ideas.

We welcome your new and more expansive ideas.

We trust that you will lead us.

We trust that it is safe to follow you.

We know you created us and that creativity

Is your nature and our own.

We ask you to unfold our lives

According to your plan, not our low self-worth.

Help us to believe that it is not too late

And that we are not too small or too flawed

To be healed—

By you and through each other—and made whole.

Help us to love one another,

To nurture each other's unfolding,

To encourage each other's growth,

And understand each other's fears.

Help us to know that we are not alone,

That we are loved and lovable.

Help us to create as an act of worship to you.

Julia Cameron

Table 7.1

DEVELOPING YOUR GIFTS
(TAKE THE GRAVE CLOTHS OFF YOUR CREATIVITY)

1. **Accept that God created gifts in you.** *"There are different kinds of gifts... he gives them to each one..." I Corinthians 12:4-6*

2. **Believe that creativity is a part of your being made in God's image.** *"Let us make man in our image, in our likeness...rule over all the earth..." Genesis 1:27*

3. **Commit to creatively develop / use your gifts for the common good, to His glory.** *"Whom I created for my glory," Isaiah 43:7; "To each is given the manifestation of the spirit for common good." I Corinthians 12:17*

4. **The refusal to be creative is self-will, motivated by fear. Confess / defy the fears.** *"In God I trust; I will not be afraid. What can man do to me?" Psalm 56:1*

5. **Creativity leads into the unknown, where there is no certainty. The resulting insecurity can be addressed by remembering Who is en route with you.** *"...Be not afraid...for the Lord your God is with you wherever you go." Joshua 1:9*

6. **Become a risk taker: let go of illusions of perfectionism and certainty.** *"...and you will be like God..." Genesis 3:5*

7. **Be willing to be in process, do badly, appear foolish, be a beginner, and / or fail.** *"He who began a good work in you will bring it to completion at the day of Jesus Christ." Philippians 1:6*

8. **Avoid sharing your creativity with those who sometimes shame you.** *"...do not throw your pearls to pigs..." Matthew 7:6*

9. **Find a supportive environment for your creative effort.** *"And let us consider how we may spur one another on toward love and good deeds." Hebrews 10:24; "...encourage one another..." I Thessalonian 5:11*

Chapter 8

Shame and Guilt

"When you make a mistake and the devil comes and tells you 'You're no good,' you don't have to take on the guilt and condemnation..."[1] Joyce Meyer

The following composite scenario is recounted in the book Shame: A Faith Perspective.[2]

Jan was an outstanding wife, mother, and member of her community. She worked part-time as a speech therapist. Her husband Mike was employed as an architect for a successful firm. This was a fine illustration of the "looking-good" family. In spite of being deemed successful from anyone's point of view, Jan often felt depressed and distressed about herself. The feelings could nose dive into such discouragement that she would see herself as a miserable failure. Despite Mike's reassurances and the encouragement from family and friends, these very negative self evaluations continued to haunt her.

One Sunday her pastor's sermon focused on the Gospel's claims of forgiveness for sin. Jan decided to meet with her pastor and share her pervasive painful feelings about herself, hoping that she simply had failed to experience true forgiveness.

The discussion with her pastor covered childhood memories such as stealing candy from a local store, high school memories such as a party that included a keg and a skinny-dipping episode. Adulthood brought forth some hateful things that she had said around inheritance issues with her sibling, a rift with Mike regarding having a second baby, and gossiping about a neighbor at a coffee party because she resented an election defeat of being a leader in the women's club.

When all the regrets that Jan could recall had been confessed, the pastor extended grace and forgiveness according to the gospel, with both of them believing that this was what she needed. A silence ensued, but soon was broken. Jan blurted out, "I feel worse than ever. I don't believe that I deserve to be forgiven. I wish I hadn't told you all of those things; now I'm not sure I can face you either." The pastor became confused as she tearfully fled from his office.

This scenario is not unusual. When forgiveness doesn't seem to work, what other dynamics are at work in the life of someone like Jan? The authors go on to suggest that the other dynamic operative in Jan's life is shame. Shame has been referred to as the overlooked and forgotten emotion. Though guilt and shame can be inextricably bound, they need to be differentiated. Knowing the difference between guilt and shame can be a good start toward managing both emotions appropriately. This chapter will explain the difference in the two emotions. Chapters that follow will offer Biblical ways to manage them.

Remember that I am defining shame as a loss of worth. Since God determines our worth, there is no occasion for a loss of our Biblically sanctioned worth. To the argument that shame acts as a deterrent to wrong doing, I respond with the reality that God's children have other deterrents to sinful choices, including guilt – one of the strongest deterrents.

So is guilt the gift that keeps on giving? And is the reason it keeps on giving because we allow it to morph into shame? I like to use the imagery of a slippery slope with shame being the diabolical pit at the base of the slippery slope. And in this discussion let us imagine guilt at the top of the slippery slope. So when guilt is not contained by responding to it appropriately, we are vulnerable for our emotional experience to take that fateful plunge right into the pit of shame.

Some of us have experienced guilt being used to control and manipulate us in our tender and formative years. The heavy, shaming reaction to our having erred may have included being scorned, mocked, exiled out of the presence of the shamer, disowned, or abandoned. And unfortunately as adults we may continue to encounter those shaming behaviors from others, as well as the proverbial guilt trip. The power lodged within a message designed to induce guilt may also carry an implication of "shame on you" lurking like a threatening storm cloud. To the extent that we have experienced this controlling device of a shame-laden guilt trip or even more blatant shame, we may have developed an association whereby being wrong is shameful. For many of us, it is a revolutionary thought that there is to be no shame, even when we have erred. And, in particular, when we have actually sinned, many of us do not know that our worth has not been altered one iota. Instead of our worth remaining unaltered, we feel that it is diminished or forfeited. When we miss the mark, we act as if we have been disrobed of the righteousness of Jesus Christ. How this must grieve the Giver of the robe of righteousness.

> *"I delight greatly in the Lord; my soul rejoices in my God. For he has clothed me with garments of salvation and arrayed me in a robe of righteousness..."*
> *Isaiah 61:10*

Thus guilt becomes layered with shame. Another way of looking at the relationship of guilt and shame is in neuroscience and the phrase credited to Carla Sharz. "Neurons that fire together wire together."[3] This being wired together means that the neuronal activity involved with the experience of being guilty fires with the neuronal activity involved with the experience of shame. In other words, it becomes automatically shameful to be guilty. So we not only suffer guilt but also the much more painful experience of loss of worth. Therefore we may become hyper-vigilant to avoid any risk of being guilty because we are ultimately avoiding a shame attack. The nature of this hyper-vigilance requires an intense focus on our deeds. When our fear of being guilty develops an obsession-like quality to it, beware. An intense determination to do the right thing can require a self-centeredness that can actually usurp our Christ-centeredness. And this self-centeredness can lead to self-righteousness. When we are finding righteousness in our ability to do the right thing, we are not relying on being robed in His righteousness. This hyper-vigilance about what we do or fail to do promotes trust in self instead of trust in God.

At this point a legitimate question may surface. Aren't we as Christians supposed to avoid sinning? Are we not supposed to avoid being guilty? Of course we are. Later we will examine Godly reasons for avoiding sin. However this hyper-vigilance to avoid guilt, which is ultimately about avoiding shame, is not what the scriptures are calling forth in our lives. Mistakes, accidents, errors, and even sinning cannot warrant shame. Our accidents, errors, and sinning may have dire consequences that we need to own and respond to. But a loss of worth is NOT one of those consequences. Whatever we reap from whatever we have sown, it is not about our worth. There is NO condemnation for those who are in Christ Jesus.

> *"Therefore there is now no condemnation for those*
> *who are in Christ Jesus." Romans 8:1*

No means no. There are no grounds for a believer to experience a loss of worth.

The ability to manage guilt Biblically is crucial to our spiritual maturity. It may also be crucial to our reduction of shame. Knowing how to manage guilt Biblically will reduce the paralyzing fear of guilt. Managing guilt according to God's instruction can free us to live life boldly, taking risks, and venturing out of comfort into discomfort. The walk of faith is not designed to be on a certain path, that is, a path of certainty – from our perspective. That's why it is called faith. So our attempts to make certain that which is uncertain, such as never being guilty, may be, at a deeper level, an attempt to avoid shame.

Writing this chapter brings up memories of my early days of motherhood. One advantage of our large family was that I was on a first name basis with the manager of the local drug store, due to the repeated phone calls to him that went something like this. "I was just in your store with my small children and one of them sneaked out with some tic tacs. I'm coming back with her to return them to you and apologize. Please take this seriously, but respectfully." My intent was to make clear the guilt and require restitution, without conveying shame on my child for her wrong doing. Shame is never needed for guiding and correcting. Not only is it not needed, shame is always destructive. (One of the advantages of being a writer, and there are few for my type of personality, is that I can illustrate from my life with a success story instead of one that, though it does not warrant shame, is full of regret prompting me to ask forgiveness and then to leave it God's hands for His redemption.)

Guilt, with its related concepts of repentance, atonement, and forgiveness is at the heart of the gospel. Our ability to live out the gospel will be impaired if we cannot manage guilt in a healthy, Biblical way.

We begin this differentiation of shame and guilt by defining guilt. The definition begins with an objective condition. We are focusing on fact – guilty or not guilty in light of something we did or failed to do. Or for people of faith, guilt may involve an internal condition, such as our thoughts or attitude. Guilt is a legal decision like a verdict rendered in our courts of law. Therefore this verdict of guilty or not guilty is unrelated to feelings. The issue is one of whether an objective rule, a law, has been breached. If someone decided to omit income from a tax return, the law requiring all income to be reported has been breached. The person is guilty. An example regarding attitude is the believer who refuses to forgive, harbors a grudge, and misses the mark set forth in scripture regarding forgiveness.

> *"See to it that no one misses the grace of God and that no bitter root grows up to cause trouble and defile many." Hebrews 12:15*

So guilt is an objective or legal condition of being guilty.

Often in my psychotherapy practice, guilt is the tormenting feeling being expressed. In order to determine the validity of guilty or not guilty, I inquire as to what sin has been committed or what law has been broken. Frequently the realization dawns that no sin nor broken law is involved. So we label this experience as false guilt and continue with an attempt to understand more of the truth of the situation.

One theme of this chapter is that Christians need to take back guilt. We have diluted its meaning rendering the experience of actually sinning or breaking a law as less clear with less meaning. Often we recognize this watering down of the concept of guilt. Consider the expression "I feel so guilty" as someone realizes the greeting of the hostess will be empty handed, without the customary hostess gift. Or "I feel so guilty that I didn't return your call sooner". We refer to the neglect of social conventions or cultural mores as grounds for guilt instead of simply acknowledging being embarrassed. I submit these common examples to suggest that the usage does not reflect the meaning of the word guilt and thereby devalues the word. With the meaning of the word diluted or trivialized, we are then at risk for losing the essence of the experience of being guilty. And, without a clear understanding of guilt, we are not likely to respond Biblically to guilt.

Since guilt is a legal decision like a verdict rendered in a court of law, the verdict is unrelated to feelings. Ultimately that verdict must be the internal work of the Holy Spirit. So when we separate guilty feelings from the dynamic and open our hearts to the possibility of being guilty, then we can experience the conviction of the Holy Spirit and respond appropriately when we are guilty.

Let us look closely at Table 8.1 that follows. The major differences in shame and guilt are outlined there.[4]

Origins:

The origins of guilt and shame differ. As previously noted, guilt needs to be based on whether we have sinned or not. In light of the law, has a law been breached? Have we missed the mark? Has the indwelling Holy Spirit rendered an objective verdict of guilty? In contrast the origin of shame is a violation of any of our personal standards that carry an automatic consequence of loss of worth. (Our personal standards, called rulebooks, will be the focus of chapter 9 where we will examine our rulebooks.) Remember that the definition of a shame attack is experiencing loss of worth. So the origin of shame (a loss of worth) is triggered by a violation of a shame-laden rule in our own rulebook. Our personal rulebook usually includes traditions that we have accumulated from places and experiences in our lives. More about our rulebook later.

When we are guilty we need to focus on something we did or failed to do or our choice of attitudes. For example we may have been hurt in a relationship, refused to forgive, and settled into an ungodly attitude of contempt toward the other. So guilt is about a choice. Whereas the focus when we are having a shame attack is on our personhood. And specifically the focus is on our value or worth as a person. A flaw within us has been exposed and we experience a loss of worth because of the exposure of that flaw. So shame regards our personhood. Shame is about us. Shame is about self. Guilt is about behavior or an attitude we harbor. It is very important to begin to see the difference in shame and guilt.

Repair:

Now the third component is the possibility of repair. If we are guilty, it is possible to be forgiven for what we did or failed to do or for an attitude. It is possible to make amends, make restitution, or to change. It is possible to avoid repeating the offense. Shame declares that we are flawed beyond repair; forgiveness is not relevant to one who is feeling worthless. We can not be forgiven for being the way we are. If the negative evaluation is about us... then... it is a done deal. I am defective. End of story. If it is about something I did then I might be able to make restitution for what I did. I might be able to make amends for what I did. I might be able to correct it. There is some hope of rectifying it, if I am focused on something I did. Hopefully the difference in shame and guilt is becoming clear. But let us continue with Table 8:1

Hope:

The next differing factor is about hope. If I am containing this experience of guilt, I can hope in the scriptural concepts of for-giveness and cleansing. I can not only count on being forgiven, I can count on being cleansed in a way that will prevent repeating the offense. The very nature of shame breeds a hopelessness about change. And that hopelessness dooms us to repeats of shame attacks.

A part of what makes a shame attack so painful is that we experience a hopelessness about ever being different; about ever experiencing worth again. Whereas, if we are focused on something that we did and how we could do it differently next time, then there is a sense of I will behave differently next time. Hope is still present.

Understanding:

Then there is the dimension of understanding. When we plunge into the pit of shame, confusion reigns. Our cognitive abilities are affected by a shame attack. Our impaired cognitive ability is best described as confusion. Sometimes we don't really know what just happened to us. All we know is that we are feeling lower than low. Whereas, if we are able to stay focused on guilt, we will be able to clarify whether we are actually guilty or not. We will even be able to enter into a redemptive process and sort out the actual sin and possibly why we yielded to some kind of temptation. We will be looking at this redemptive process in chapter 10.

Feelings:

The feelings associated with guilt and those with shame differ this way. Shame is an affect in and of itself. And this painful affect or emotion is overwhelming. Whereas the condition of being guilty is unrelated to feelings. We may experience remorse. Being under conviction of being guilty may be accompanied by sad feelings. Or the accompanying emotion may be described as Godly sorrow.

"Godly sorrow brings repentance that leads to salvation..." 2 Corinthians 7: 10

But the feelings may not be present, or if they are present, they do not need to be overwhelming or devastating. If the remorse is quite intense, this is a red flag for the guilt having morphed into shame. This is particularly true because of the next differentiating factor.

Power:

Again the very nature of shame is to overwhelm, confuse, and render us powerless over the experience. We seem powerless over the confusion, over remembering what worth felt like, over any hope for ever feeling worth again. We seem absolutely powerless over the loss of worth. However, containing the experience to guilty leaves us empowered to respond appropriately. We can begin to remember the Biblical instructions for responding to guilt, which will be treated in detail in chapter 10. The awareness that the forgiveness is already provided can motivate us to access that forgiveness. Remembering that repentance and restoration are God's will for us is empowering.

Forgiveness:

Being forgiven for failing to measure up to the rest of the human race seems unforgivable. It does not make much sense to be forgiven for being worthless. Again forgiveness is irrelevant to our experience of shame. Whereas focusing on a deed or an attitude makes forgiveness relevant. Knowing the forgiveness provided that day on a hill called Calvary creates an opportunity to partake of the forgiveness or not.

> *"When you were dead in your sins and in the uncir-*
> *cumsicion of your sinful nature, God made you alive*
> *with Christ. He forgave us all our sins, having can-*
> *celed the written code, with its regulations, that was*
> *against us and that stood opposed to us; he took it*
> *away nailing it to the cross." Colossians 2:13-14*

Motivation:

And then there is a difference in shame and guilt regarding motivation. Our primary motivation during a shame attack is to hide. We wish we could hide from everybody. And that includes the wish to hide from God. And, of course that tendency to hide from God means we are hiding from His grace. When we can recognize and own our guilt, we can proceed to confession. We can follow the scriptural provision to access the incredible grace of God. Confessing to the offended party and to God ushers us into His grace. We are then in a posture to receive forgiveness and experience His grace.

Dynamic:

Again, the dynamic is one of staying at the top of the slope and containing guilt to guilt. We have been provided forgiveness. We have been provided a process for being forgiven and cleansed. By entering into this process, we can avoid the hellish plunge into the diabolical pit of shame. Whatever we have done or failed to do does not warrant a loss of worth. However sinful we feel convicted that we have been, no sin can touch our worth. God, our creator, determined our worth. He designed our worth to be from His hand and of His heart. Our worth is unrelated to our sinful behaviors. (I can never pen these words without a hallelujah rising within me.) He knows the sinful condition of our hearts. He declared His love and our worth to be unaffected by any sinful attitude harbored in our secret places. The worst case scenario is that we sin against Him. We grieve Him when we take life into our own hands. He yearns for complete trust in His goodness. He delights in our obedience for many reasons. There are wonderful reasons for trusting and obeying. But our inherent worth in God's eyes is not earned by obedience. So when our obedience is shown to have lapsed, when we miss the mark, we need to immediately enter into the Biblical process of responding to the condition of being guilty. Among the benefits of entering into this process is avoiding a shame attack.

A shame attack typically comes on suddenly and unexpectedly. The essence of shame is an exposure of our defectiveness laid bare for all to see. It is as if the whole world perceives our defect. We are victimized by our worst nightmare. Now any that care to gaze can enjoy a panoramic view of the world's greatest phony. The charade is over. The masquerade is over. Our sinful or finite nature becomes completely transparent. Is it any wonder that shame is considered the most painful experience amongst the human emotions?

An analogy of managing guilt can be drawn to managing anger. Scripture warns us to appropriately manage our anger, lest we sin and /or allow it to develop into bitterness.

"In your anger do not sin..." Ephesians 4:26

"See to it that no one misses the grace of God and that no bitter root grows up to cause trouble and defile many." Hebrews 12: 15

Likewise responding to guilt in a God-directed way will prevent more suffering than is necessary. We can resolve guilt so that it is not the gift that keeps on giving – so that guilt does not lower or annihilate our sense of Biblically-ordained worth. If we, as believers, develop the ability to contain guilt to guilt, not allowing the guilt to plunge us into the pit of shame, we can more effectively live out the gospel.

Now that we have reviewed the difference in shame and guilt, we need to understand the Biblical way to respond to guilt. The way of responding based on Biblical truths will enable us to contain guilt to guilt. Table 10.3 in chapter 10 is an outline of shame-free repentance contrasted with shame-based repentance. But first, in the next chapter, let us begin to consider the role that idolatry can play in our experiences of shame attacks.

Table 8.1

	Shame	Guilt
SHAME vs. GUILT		
Origin	Violation of own rulebook	Sin
Focus	On me, my person-hood	On something I did / failed to do or my attitude
Repair	Beyond forgiveness	Forgivable
Hope	Hopeless about ever being different	To be cleansed, avoid repeat
Understanding	Too confused to know what happened	Clarity re: the yielding to the temptation
Feelings	Of shame overwhelm	Legal condition regardless of feelings
Power	Powerless over the experience	Empowered to respond appropriately
Forgiveness	Seems unforgivable	Desire to seek it
Motivation	To hide from everybody, includes God which excludes His grace	To confess to offended one, to God, and be graced
Dynamic	Diabolical pit, bottom of slope	Top of slippery slope

Chapter 9

Shame and Idolatry

"The dearest idol I have known,
Whate'er that idol be,
Help me to tear it from thy throne,
And worship only thee."

(From a hymn by William Cowper)

For most of the now many years that my husband and I have attended church, we have often referred to a classic old joke. In fact the reference to it became one of those moments whereby the punch line is conveyed by just a look we shoot one to the other. The joke has an elderly man and his wife dutifully listening to a sermon. (Picture a Norman Rockwell scene.) As the minister develops his spiritual commentary, reaching a particularly convicting place in his message, the gentleman leans over and whispers to his wife, "Now he's stopped preaching and gone to meddling."

Perhaps the title of this chapter tempts us to dread some meddling. We may timidly approach this chapter because the word idolatry is daunting. But in fact the discovery of anything in our lives that calls for repentance is good news. By the very nature of repentance, we have an opportunity to draw closer to God, trusting in His mercy, seeking and receiving His forgiveness. This means of experiencing His grace deepens our ability to trust him. It is a means of transformation. When a child of God repents, God is beautifully glorified. So let us approach the relationship between idolatry and shame with anticipation that something good this way comes.

The word idolatry may be restricted in its meaning to the golden calves worshipped by the Israelites. But the jealousy of God declared in Exodus 20 requires us to expand the concept of idolatry to understanding that over-attachment to anything constitutes abominations of our heart. Idolatry is in full force when certain objects, practices, relationships, or achievements have become more our Savior than Christ. When something in addition to the work and provision of Jesus is sought after because it is deemed as important, as needful for increasing our worth, then our desire has crossed that fine line into idolatry.

Few students of shame have written about this key and pivotal dynamic of the relationship of shame and idolatry. I am indebted to Dan Allender for his profound contribution to the subject of shame, and, especially, its relationship to idolatry. My pastor at Fourth Presbyterian Church in Bethesda, Maryland, Dr. Robert Norris, has also contributed to my understanding of the role idolatry plays in the experience of shame.

Let us begin our exploration of shame's relationship to idolatry in the following narrative, Table 9.1, with these introductory comments. The development of idolatry in our lives is depicted in the following narrative as a pursuit of worth. In the beginning, in God's creative will, He created us and declared His creation to be very good. And then the rest of scripture expounds on the worth that God placed on us, right on up through the historical sacrificial life, death, and resurrection of Jesus Christ for our eternal salvation. After the ascension of Christ, The Holy Spirit came to indwell us and be a constant infusion of the worth God extends to us. He designed us with a crucial need to know that worth. He clearly intended to meet that need for knowing our worth. So crucial is this need to experience worth, whatever we perceive as giving us worth – we will worship that source of worth. God planned to be our source of worth. And so our looking to any other source for obtaining, maintaining a sense of our worth leads us into idolatry because we will worship a source of worth, whether that source is legitimate or illegitimate. The narrative that follows begins with several interchangeable expressions of worth. This material will continue using worth as the antithesis of shame. You are encouraged to substitute any of the listed synonyms for worth that resonate best in your heart as the antithesis for shame. So this God-given need of worth is established as so intrinsically crucial to our well-being, that it is a life and death issue. As we read the narrative in Table 9.1 part 1 and part 2 about shame's relationship to idolatry, may it deepen our understanding of how prone we are toward idolatry.

The narrative, Table 9.1, about the life and death issue of having a source of worth, a means for experiencing ourselves as valuable, serves as an introduction to The Idol System, Table 9.2. Understanding the components of our idol system is essential to the healing process. You will notice that the idol is the center of this system.

But let's start at the upper left quadrant of Table 9.2 This condition of our flesh discussed in chapter 1 is the carnal desire to be like God – primarily the desire to be in control. Specifically, this is innate shame. We are born with this desire as a part of our flesh. Our sinful nature carries this legacy. And this desire to be in control will always be among our desires this side of heaven. Even the most mature followers of Christ imaginable have an ongoing reckoning with this part of their inheritance, of their nature. In complete honesty can we not recognize, perhaps deep within or maybe not so deep within, that tendency to resist our finiteness? We want to say to others, you can be finite. But I want to be the human exception. Finiteness is too limiting. Surely if I overreach in some arena, I can pull it off. Surely I can defy my limits, my imperfections. We not only refuse to accept our finiteness, we are ashamed of it. When it gets exposed, we may very well have a shame attack. And yet scripture holds out hope that we will rejoice in our inheritance.

"Instead of their shame my people will receive a double portion, and instead of disgrace the they will rejoice in their inheritance..." Isaiah 61: 7

Can we imagine rejoicing in our finiteness? So this inborn desire to control is the beginning of what will eventually become our idol system.

The next quadrant in Table 9.2 is the lower left one that recognizes God's design of us finite beings as having a need for worth. This intrinsic, intense desire is actually a God-given need. God designed us to need to know our worth. In fact the need for worth can hardly be overstated. He wanted us to know that we are valuable, special, and significant. The entirety of the Bible is one colossal love letter. His creation and relationship with man depicted in Genesis reveals His unmistakable pleasure in us. He began to have an intimate relationship with these finite beings. The communion they were privileged to have as they walked in the garden everyday was palpably sweet. He designed His relationship with us to be one that daily infused us with worth. That kind of intimacy with our Creator would be a lifeline that conveyed significance, belonging, value. We would have no doubts about our worth. And in return, we would worship our source of worth. This, my friends, was paradise.

Moving to the upper right quadrant of The Idol System in Table 9.2, we see that deception arrives on the scene. Embodied in the evil one's treachery is a lie. The essence of the lie is that there is more worth available than God extended to us. We only need to pursue it. The sine qua non of Satan's deceit was that God was withholding something good that is needed and can be obtained by human effort. Matthew Henry describes Satan's strategy with Adam and Eve:

> *"...he aims to beget in them, 1. Discontent with their present state, as if it were not so good as it might be, and should be... 2. Ambition of preferment, as if they were fit to be gods. Satan had ruined himself by desiring to be like the Most High, Isa. 14:14, therefore seeks to infect our first parents with the same desire, that he might ruin them too."*[1]

Thus the pursuit of becoming infinite like God was launched. Rooted in this fundamental lie is the deception that there are other attainable sources of worth apart from God. And like Adam and Eve, we also are deceived. Not only do we think we can attain more worth, we also think we can secure it from a source other than our Creator.

And then the final quadrant of the idol system in Table 9.2, the lower right one, is our rule book[2]. Now the idol system takes on a personal component. Our rulebooks vary from one person to another according to the particular rules we have constructed over the years. Remember the trial and shame-filled error in Table 9.1. Our rules emerged according to the behaviors we hoped would deliver a sense of worth. They are our own personal rules that we believe are right and necessary and possible. This set of rules corresponds to or supports the particular idol(s) in our idol system. At this point let us consider idol in the plural. For most of us find our idolatry involves more than one idol. So the rules, called the *shoulds* of life, form our rule book.

Typically our rules are written in the *should format*. Beginning a rule with "I should..." may seem innocent enough. Beware. This format is far from benign. The implication of any statement beginning with "I should..." is two-fold, regarding both failure and success. The failure to carry out the established *should* carries the penalty "shame on you!". Successfully obeying the "should" promises worth. The two-fold implication is lodged in the rulebook, sometimes hidden, always motivating. This implication is the proverbial coin with two sides. One side implies the penalty for failure to abide by the rule – loss of worth (shame). The other side implies that obeying this rule enhances our worth.

When I first began developing this material to present in seminars, I realized that relying on our rules was not only NOT God's intent for us, but that it was a diabolic strategy to interfere with experiencing God's grace. In this horrific realization I decided the word should is better spelled *shud* so that it becomes a four letter word. Of course the word processor objected to the word shud. It recommended scud. I recognized this word as the name of a surface to air missile and related that weaponry to the *shuds* in terms of effect. The impact of a violated "shud" is as if we launch a missile to our very own souls or to the soul of others when we are shaming them. By the end of this chapter, notice if you agree with making should a four letter word.

Listed in Table 9.3 are examples of the *shuds* that might comprise our rule book. Some of our rules may be explicit and intentional. Others may be more covert, but nevertheless, influencing our behaviors. This is not an exhaustive list. But they are good examples of the rules that we establish – the rules that govern so much of our behaviors. In addition to conscious choices, behavior that is performed without much thought comes from the governance of these rules also. And the function of keeping these rules is to appease an idol in order to obtain a sense of our worth. Since these rules are framed with "I should...", the implication is "shame on me if I don't" and "I will earn my worth if I do".

The first group has to do with "looking good". We expect to maintain this "looking good" image by making everything in life perfect. This is perfectionism across the board. The list describes additional ways we count on looking good, such as being liked by everyone, never making a mistake (note the finite issues), always being rational and fair, and always saying the correct thing. Those are some of the most common kinds of *shuds* found in the dynamic of perfectionism.

The next group is one that a lot of people are very familiar with – it especially flourishes in the Christian community. We have assumed some ideas of these rules as being biblically submissive, as being godly behaviors. So we are quite vulnerable for adopting these behaviors as a part of our idolatrous system. Do any of these listed under "Being Submissive" seem familiar? I should never rock the boat, never speak up and express my opinion, never argue, make others feel good at my expense. (At my expense is crucial in that line. It is called de-selfing.) We continue with the possible appeasing behaviors such as take care of all situations where someone else feels bad, make the peace, not allow people to argue or fight, always take the least part, give everything and put my needs aside. It is a good description of what we call co-dependency. This is pretty much giving up having a self. What an affront to our Creator!

The next section is focused on feelings, previously discussed in chapter 4. I should never get angry. When this *shud* makes our rule-book, we will have shame around the fact that we have anger. No doubt actually being angry, especially expressing anger will be make us vulnerable for a shame attack. Women may be more likely to have experienced shame about expressing anger. Typically for men the more shamed emotion may be hurt. A little boy responding to distress with tears has often been deemed unacceptable, which shames the feelings of sadness and /or hurt. But male and female clients who bravely struggle with their relationship to their own emotions often discover they were required to put on a happy face regardless of what was going on inside them. Whenever any emotion is deemed unacceptable and not allowed that emotion is being shamed. Every time a child is required to deny what he is really feeling a layer of shame gets wrapped around that feeling. Additionally, an emotion gets shamed when a child's role model pretends a certain feeling does not exist or acts embarrassed if that feeling is showing. Thus we as children may have learned that certain feelings are shameful.

The last group in Table 9.3 is also very common. I *shud* always be strong and never ill. Lots of people struggle with calling in for a sick day, even though they are clearly sick. Our society is characterized as too autonomous, too self-sufficient. Many of us have a lot of difficulty asking for help because of our be-strong image that we are endeavoring to maintain. We are determined to keep any health issue from interfering with our responsibilities. Be healthy and energetic always. Always! We continue to fulfill our responsibilities until there is not an ounce of energy left in us. I have an electronic device and the battery is supposed to be drained each time it is used. This is what a lot of us do to ourselves. We start giving and we give until the battery is dead because I must rescue those who are in trouble. Or I must carry out all my duties all by myself. This is just a smattering of the kind of rules that we have developed within our selves, creating the rule book that the judge uses. Remember de judge? Here come de judge... "shame, shame, shame." This is the rulebook that de judge uses to declare shame upon us, divesting us of our worth.

Much can be said of the ungodly nature of these rules. They are inhumane in the use of *always* and *never*. They defy our finiteness by tempting us toward perfectionism. Our rules seduce us away from the reality that perfection is not possible. They misrepresent God as requiring perfection. Thus we risk setting higher standards than those of our Father. Additionally a focus on our being perfect would require a self absorption that is not biblical. Furthermore, the effort to make no mistake is dangerous. Paradoxically, those of us with this rule live as if it is dangerous to make a mistake. But a look at the passage of scripture regarding the ten talents reminds us that our creator is clearly interested in our investing, which by definition carries risk. (See Matthew 25:14-29.) Only by claiming a freedom to err, to fail, can we ever move toward living a life aligned with the original plan. So not only does cautious living, designed to be error free, not reflect the freedom meant for God's children, it deadens our potential to grow into the unique child He created in the first place.

Please turn to Table 9.3, remembering that these *shuds* are an essential part of the idol system. The violation of a *shud* is a necessary trigger for a shame attack. At least one violated rule is always involved in a shame attack. The failure to obey or carry out a *shud* is the basis *de judge* uses for rendering a verdict of shame on you.

Our shame attacks reflect our rules. Previously we saw that *de judge* who dwells within declares "shame, shame, shame" based on our rule books. The pivotal point of the shame attack is the violation of a *shud*, a rule sitting smugly and self-righteously in our rule book. Our *shuds* are the heavy hand of the law. The law leads to death. The law is not about grace.

173

"Clearly no one is justified before God by the law, because,'The righteous will live by faith'."
Galatians 3:11

The law is about a standard that I can and must measure up to… and, shame if I don't! Each of us has our own personalized version of a rule book. And often we are not aware of its contents. Usually we work backwards to discover a *shud* in our rule book. As we will see in chapter 12, we start with a shame attack and as we seek healing, the rule that we have violated is revealed to us in the healing process. Once we are aware of the rule, we can then decide against it and relinquish it in the healing process.

"When I was a child, I talked like a child, I thought like a child, I reasoned like a child. When I became a man, I put childish ways behind me." I Corinthians 13:11

And so the idol system is complete. It starts with our beginning – both our natural craving to be in control, to be as God, and our natural, God-given need for worth. With that both godly and ungodly beginning, we add the deception that worth can be accessed from some source other than our Creator. Then the system takes on personal and individual components as we chose idols, our sources of worth, and the appeasing rules required by those particular idols. This source of pseudo-worth will eventually, by the mercy of God, fail us so intensely and consistently, creating an opportunity for us to move from shame to glory. The pursuits of this pseudo-worth will be revealed as a tormenting, savage attack on our souls.

Now what might an idol system look like? The examples in Table 9.4 are some very common systems of idolatry. As you read Table 9.4 notice that each of the following examples names an idol, states the supportive lie, and some probable appeasing behavior that is required in a particular idol system. Note that the supportive lie is always about the pursuit of worth and avoiding shame. The appeasing *shuds* are simply possibilities of the behaviors we may have adopted to serve our particular idols. These examples are to aid our understanding of the idol system and can be very useful in the healing process. The ultimate benefit of this list is to help us be open to the Lord revealing to us our own personal idol system. Being willing to be convicted of our idol system is a crucial part of the healing process. Please read Table 9.4 and my commentary on these examples.

The first one in Table 9.4 is performance. Basically this embodies the idea that those who perform the best are worth the most. The lie that supports the idol in this idol system is "I only have worth and avoid shame if my performance is flawless." To appease the idol of performance, we may attempt to make no mistakes, no errors, show no weaknesses or inexperience, never be a novice; perform perfectly or don't perform. These *shuds* have to do with avoiding a flaw or letting anybody know about a flaw. Cover it over, blame someone else, shift the attention elsewhere, whatever it takes to appease the idol of performance. These behaviors of appeasing an idol actually hold us captive. Thus the idol system is a prison. When our idol system is working, we deny the emptiness and the shame despite the success. By this is meant that even when we are succeeding, the success has a hollow feel to it. The worth we are experiencing is fragile and transient. Then when the idol fails us, the emptiness and the shame can become a full-blown shame attack. Occasionally God allows this emptiness to surface during the success of appeasing an idol. And that may be that well known despondent question, "Is this all there is?"

The next example is achievement. "I only have worth and avoid shame if I am being recognized for my accomplishments." This one usually finds people striving for status, recognition, and taking credit for anything good that is happening anywhere near them. They are not helping others to succeed. In fact their behaviors keep others unsuccessful or inferior in some way. Do not get in this person's way if you are attempting to achieve something. Do not ask for some attention to be turned toward you. At best you will be seen as an inconvenience. At worst you will be blamed for any setback, much less failure or utter ruin that they may experience.

I have already referred to number 3 at some length. Faux peace is when we give up parts of who we are in order to keep the peace. The effort to avoid conflict and troublesome feelings is usually seen as being nice. Under that definition, we recognize nice to be a four-letter word. This idol requires keeping everything positive. The behaviors that appease this idol reap constant affirmation by those who hold

176

tightly to the utopian illusion that life is supposed to be pleasant and peaceful. Again, though accolades are plentiful, there will be emptiness and shame despite success. Even when compulsively being a nice person seems to be working, if we look deep in our hearts, we know there is still emptiness there, beneath the ill-gotten worth.

For illustrative purposes at this point, I usually show this cartoon of a guy standing at the seat of judgment with the pearly gates in the background. His is pleading for his eternal destiny saying, "But I attended every National Prayer Breakfast." We can imagine that he was either operating in the idolatrous system of performance or achievement, or how about both?

Number 4 in Table 9.4 is a very common idol and again, the operative word is flawless. "I only have worth and avoid shame if my character is flawless." Now what might this involve? Most likely it involves all that sinful stuff, and that finite stuff that is unacceptable to us. And so, we must be above all of that such as revenge, jealousy, lust, and idolatry. We would never have gossip, meanness, rebellion, self-absorption, insensitivity, rudeness, etc. be in our lives. Even to be capable of acting out of these flaws may threaten our sense of our worth. These flaws must absolutely not be any part of our capability. This idol is boldly represented in the Pharisee who was praying in the temple. He was not merely thanking God that he had not committed the sins that the other man was confessing. Read the verse carefully. He was thanking God that he was not like that other man.

"The Pharisee stood up and prayed about himself: 'God, I thank you that I am not like all other men— robbers, evildoers, adulterers—or even like this tax collector...But the tax collector would not even look up to heaven, but beat his breast and said, 'God, have mercy on me, a sinner'." Luke 18: 11-13

This idolatrous system is the breeding ground for assumptions that our nature does not even have the capability, much less the tendency, for exhibiting any flaws of character. The word religion is included in the name of this idol because religious rationalizations so often accompany this display of supposed flawless character.

The next example of an idol system, number 5, represents a gift from God. But we get seduced into worshipping the gift instead of the giver. Family is certainly designed and created by God as a way for us to live, to function, to procreate, a way for us to have community. Sometimes I observe those God-given blessings enticing us into idolatry. These gifts that originate out of God's bounty become increasingly cherished until at some point, we cross that fine line into idolatry. Sarah Young expresses this concept so well in her devotional, *Jesus Calling*, when she conveys God's heart:

"Though I delight in blessing my children, I am deeply grieved when my blessings become idols in their heart."[3]

Frequently at this point in the seminar, attendees are wondering how to prevent affections for blessings and successes from crossing that fine line into idolatry. My response to that is to be sure to give themselves the freedom to enjoy and delight in God's goodness. Know that God wants us to rejoice with Him. He is the kind of God who throws a party so we can savor his goodness.

> *"Bring the fattened calf and kill it. Let's have a feast*
> *and celebrate." Luke 15:23*

And then when you have experienced and expressed your joy and gratitude, remind yourself – this goodness has nothing to do with my worth. My worth is the same after being blessed with success as it was in the midst of failure. My worth is not altered by anything I do or fail to do. Thank you, God.

Continuing with Table 9.4, lordship you notice, is with a small case "L". Again, we are back to the idea of power and control that is beyond realistic expectations for a finite human being. This is the person who is not going to get surprised, who is not going to be absolutely baffled by something that happens. These are the people that order their lives to rule out uncertainty and surprises. They can even figure out God. If they have a moment where they cannot explain God, they are going to be angry until He answers their "why" question.

Attachment, number 7, has some similarity to family. It is about being overly attached to someone or a group and that attachment becomes a source of worth.

Number 8, suffering, may be surprising. Read it carefully to understand how idolatry can be related to suffering.

Another very common one is number 9, approval. If we have the idol of approval, people's approval is pursued as a source of worth. Sometimes just one or two people are singled out. If their approval is our idol, then we certainly fear losing that approval from them. And so, we fear man and become very focused on man, and forget about a good fear, fearing God. One of the quotes displayed on a poster during the seminar presentation refers to this idol:[4]

> *"Only the fear of God can deliver us from the fear of man." John Witherspoon*

Scripture is replete with warnings about this idol commonly called people pleasing.

> *"They loved praise from men more than praise from God." John 12:43*

The last one in Table 9.4 that I will mention is number 11, helping. This one also may be surprising. This is where we encourage people to be dependent on us and need us. "I should scan the environment for needs; set up a hotline, go above and beyond any request; do for them, versus teaching how it is done; have no requirements of the helpee; act put off or accuse of ingratitude if the helpee attempts to be independent of the helper. This is another illustration of a godly notion slipping across that fine line into idolatry. It is a Godly concept, certainly, of being a servant, of being an instrument of God, to love people, to have people feel God's love through us. And yet, we take this Godly concept and we create an idol out of it. And so then we are on that treadmill. We have to serve and appease the taskmaster, the very hard taskmaster. Mercy is missing in all the dynamics of idolatry. We certainly are called to be God's feet and hands. But we are not to start assuming that our worth is related to how He uses us to bless others.

So how does our idol system manifest itself in our choices and our motivations? What does it look like to be imprisoned in an idol system? In fact there is a pattern of this treadmill lifestyle. And it shows up in terms of a pattern of motivations and behaviors. The pattern, in Table 9.5, is best conceptualized in a cycle. This will be a familiar cycle for even casual students of The Old Testament. Concisely, there we see God's chosen people slip into idolatry, get oppressed by an enemy, cry out to God, get delivered, prosper, and slip back into idolatry. So Table 9.5 presents these dynamics in a circular graph. We will examine this cycle starting at the top.

The idolatry is ruling our motivations and choices in this part of the cycle. Whatever we have pursued in order to experience our worth and value is a successful pursuit. We have no issue with feeling insignificant or less than those around us. This is a time of pseudo soul prosperity. And then, eventually in God's mercy, he allows the idol to fail.

"Their heart is divided; now shall they be found faulty: he shall break down their altar, he shall spoil their images." Hosea 10:2, (The King James Version)

(Move down on the right in the circular graph.) That which was supplying our worth either malfunctions or ceases to exist. Perhaps the idol system was centered around a job that not only provided income but also had become a source of worth that we had craved. So the notorious pink slip arrives and the source of worth is gone. Now there is way more to this trial if the job had crossed that fine line into idolatry. This is an intensely challenging time without any idolatry involved. But for one where the job was an idol, this loss is devastating! So much more is lost than a source of income. So much more is lost than a job that was a good fit, and therefore enjoyable. Remembering that worth is a life and death issue, when the idol fails, there is a severing of a lifeline. And that severed lifeline creates devastation that embodies a full-blown shame attack.

Dropping down to the shame attack part of the cycle, we see the tendency to flee from God. Sometimes this part of the cycle includes anger at God and becomes a crisis of faith. The essence of experiencing a shame attack is a desperation and a hopelessness about this sense of worthlessness.

Eventually hope begins to stir. However it is not a faith-based hope. It is a hope grounded in human ingenuity and effort. By definition the idolatry lives on. And so without a Godly resolution of the faith crisis, there is a recommitment to the idol, noted in the cycle. The motivation may sound like this: "I will get a replacement. And it will be all that I used to have and maybe even more. I will try harder. Now I know what I *shud* do to make this all I need it to be. I can do this and I will do this." When the next job is offered, it has already been fashioned into the idolatrous soul as the key to worth. The demands of that idolatrous soul are in full force rationalizing that the key to worth has been found. And so at the bottom of the cycle, we again see the idol supplying worth.

Again, at some point, God's mercy shows up to expose the idolatry. In some manner the idol begins to fail in supplying worth. Perhaps the job is gone again or disillusionment sets in, dispelling the illusion that it could be a source of the needed intrinsic worth. A shame attack will ensue.

Moving up the left side of the cycle, notice a change in the next stage. The change may simply be a replacement of the idol. In the example we are using, there may be a decision that what the soul deeply longs for is not to be found in a job. But it will be found in a potential idol such as family. This phase of the cycle may sound like this: "I'll just get a make-do job. It will supply an income and that is all. BUT I will be committed to my family. I will be more involved with my loved ones. And there I will find the meaning of my life. Then all will be well with my soul." (Beware family! You may be in for a kind of love and commitment that does not feel very cherishing.) And so the fresh commitment based in human cleverness and effort is in full swing. The energy is applied to the treadmill. And the cycle goes on – The Cycle of Christian Carnality.

Is there another way? Are we doomed to live as the Israelites, cycling from idolatry, to being dejected, to being rescued, to prospering, and to slipping into idolatry again? Notice that when they were prospering they slipped into idol worship. No, we are not bound in such slavery depicted by this Christian carnality cycle. Continue with me. An alternate cycle is on the horizon – coming in the next chapter. The alternate cycle represents sanctification or transformation. It is a picture of spiritual growth. It is a cycle of deepening trust and increasing intimacy with God. Also in the next chapter we have an opportunity to see in scripture some of the heart of God toward us. And this understanding of God's heart will be very useful, if not absolutely necessary, in the healing process

---

Table 9.1

SHAME AND IDOLATRY

PART 1

My soul

was created

needing

WORTH

{
Value
To belong
To know it's good that I am
To know I'm supposed to be here
Being special
Being loved / lovable
Purpose
Significance

Without which—
I would have been too shamed to live…
Which makes it **a life and death issue.**

I had to satisfy this need at any price, at any cost—life versus death! Unfortunately, I inherited a tendency to satisfy this need apart from my Creator. At a tender age, I knew, and, yet completely unaware, I must find this source of life on my own and determined to do so.

Since I was destined to worship that which would—provide my worth and save me from the deadly shame…this was a quest for an idol.

Soon I choose one, the idol I had the most hope of appeasing…and, I struck a bargain:
By trail and shame-filled error I would discover the rules I should keep for serving / worshipping / appeasing my idol…while begin supplied the worth that I craved. Should I violate a rule, the idol would cut off my supply of worth, leaving me helplessly, hopelessly in that deadly shame.

So young, yet wise enough to hide all this in the dark part of my heart, Lest I be found worshipping this god. So, I look back and ask myself, "How has 'the bargain' worked out?"

Table 9.1

SHAME AND IDOLATRY

PART 2

My idol is a hard task master, always has been…but so worth it!

Although I have continued all these years to discover more rules, I do look forward to the day that I'll know all the rules. Then, if I try really hard, I'm sure I'll be able to do what I should do all the time. Then…no more shame, deadly shame. **And, it will be so worth it.**

Occasionally I have doubts about ever knowing all the rules…especially when I'm suddenly back in the shame again, desperately trying to figure out yet another rule that will appease the idol. Got to have that worth! It's a life and death issue, you know.

So it has to be worth it. Besides…is there any other way.

"…This is what the Sovereign LORD says; Repent! Turn from your idols and renounce all your detestable practices!" Ezekiel 15:6

"…If we confess our sins, he is faithful and just and will forgive us our sins and purify us from all unrighteousness." 1 John 1:9

"See, I lay a stone in Zion, a chosen and precious cornerstone, and the one who trusts in him will never be put to shame." 1 Peter 2:6

"Come to Me all you who labor and are heavily burdened,…you will find rest for your souls; for My yoke is easy and My burden is light." Matthew 11:28-29

"This righteousness from God comes through faith in Jesus Christ to all who believe…" Romans 3:22

"And my God will supply every need of yours according to his riches in glory in Christ Jesus." Philippians 4:19

"But now he has reconciled you by Christ's physical body through death to present you holy in his sight without blemish and free from accusation." Colossians 1:22

"Therefore, there is now no condemnation for those who are in Christ Jesus." Romans 8:1

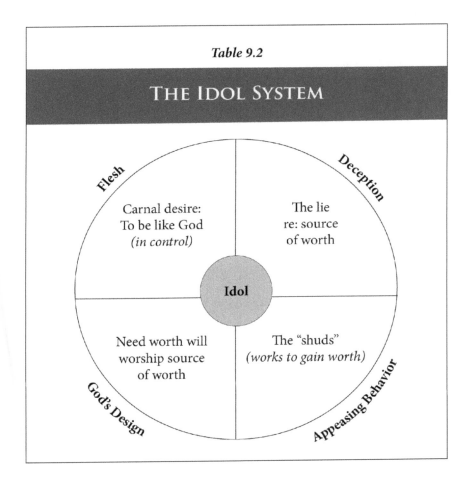

Table 9.2

THE IDOL SYSTEM

Flesh

Carnal desire:
To be like God
(in control)

Deception

The lie
re: source
of worth

Idol

Need worth will
worship source
of worth

God's Design

The "shuds"
(works to gain worth)

Appeasing Behavior

Table 9.3

THE "SHUDS"—BEING PERFECT

I should always look good.

...make everything in my life perfect or I am a failure.

...always be liked by everyone.

...never make a mistake.

...always be rational and fair while others are allowed to lose their heads.

...always say the correct thing.

Being Submissive

I should never rock the boat.

...never speak up and express my opinion.

...never argue with those in authority.

...make others feel good at my expense.

...take care of all situations where someone else feels bad.

...make the peace and not allow people to argue or fight.

...always take the least part.

...give everything and put my needs aside.

Not Allowing Feelings

I should never get angry.

...deal in thoughts and not emotions.

...never talk about how unhappy I am.

...deny my feelings when others express strong emotions and deprecate me.

Being Strong

I should always be strong.

...never be ill.

...never ask for help.

...do it all by myself.

...always be healthy and energetic.

I must continue taking care of others until I am depleted.

...rescue those who are in trouble.

Table 9.4

EXAMPLES OF IDOL SYSTEMS

PART 1

The idol / supportive lie / appeasing "shuds"

1. **Performance:** "I only have worth and avoid shame if my performance is flawless." Make no mistake, no errors; show no weakness, inexperience; never be a novice; perform perfectly or don't perform, deny emptiness regardless of success.

2. **Achievement:** "I only have worth and avoid shame if I am being recognized for my accomplishments." Strive for status, ensure recognition, get credit for any good around me, keep others under me; shame anything / anyone obstructing my agenda, deny emptiness regardless of success.

3. **Faux Peace:** "I only have worth and avoid shame if I can keep the peace." Be "nice;" avoid negativity, differentness, conflicts, troublesome feelings; rescue negative conversation, deny emptiness regardless of success.

4. **Character / religion:** "I only have worth and avoid shame if my character is flawless." Be above revenge, jealousy, lust, idolatry, gossip, meanness, rebellion, self-absorption, insensitivity, rudeness, shallowness, appearing weak in any way, depressed, hurt, unspiritual, petty, unloving, angry, fearful, lonely, needy, wanting attention / praise / encouragement; be fearful of sinning or condescending about sin *(both suggest I am above sinning)*, deny emptiness regardless of success.

5. **Family:** "I only have worth and avoid shame if family or one member is flawless." Get married, stay married, have children, obligate each to keep the family looking-good, stay together, shame member who risks tainting the image or anyone / anything suggesting a flaw, deny / defend wrong behavior, deny emptiness regardless of success.

6. **Lordship:** "I only have worth and avoid shame if I can be like God." Guess, predict, rationalize till the uncertain seems certain; take no risks; analyze everyone including God to eliminate surprises; deny insecurity by believing in absolute cause and effect; avoid the gray unknown by seeing all as black or white; avoid walking by the spirit by creating rules to live by; avoid vulnerability by asking questions and focusing on the other; dominate the conversation so it stays safe for me; be whatever gets compliance *(sweet, strong, angry)*; shame anyone's non-compliance, deny emptiness regardless of success.

7. **Attachment:** "I only have worth and avoid shame if someone is there to protect me and keep me safe." Avoid risk of abandonment; never develop an identity *(use another's)* never practice autonomy *(be compliant)*; insist the other stay focused on me or vice versa; guilt trip them for other interests; limit their potential for growth; never admit any flaw or be totally flawed *(incapable)*; insist on life & death need of them; deny any dependence or insist that dependence is legitimate, deny emptiness regardless of success.

189

Table 9.4

EXAMPLES OF IDOL SYSTEMS

PART 2

8. **Suffering:** "I only have worth and avoid shame if I am hurting because being a problem makes me worthy of love." See the glass as half empty, focus on the sad, offensive or fearful aspects of the situation, ignore blessings, abstain from giving thanks, settle for pity instead of love, deny emptiness regardless of success.

9. **Approval:** "I only have worth and avoid shame if I am loved and respected by _____." Adopt the other's likes / dislikes; mind-read to meet expectation; be vigilant to meet needs before expressed; never hold other accountable, always affirm OR insist on other's approval, punish for disapproval. Most effective in combination with #1 and #4, deny emptiness regardless of success.

10. **Control:** "I only have worth and avoid shame if I am able to master one area of my life." Do whatever it takes to control this area or agonize about lack of control; use self-mastery, vs. support from others. Speak of this often to stay motivated; give no one including God credit for any success; deny emptiness regardless of success.

11. **Helping:** "I only have worth and avoid shame if people are dependent on me and need me." Scan the environment for needs; set up hotline; go above and beyond any request; just do it vs. teaching how it's done; have no requirements of the one being helped; act put off or accuse of ingratitude if the one being helped attempts independence, deny emptiness regardless of success.

12. **Work:** "I only have worth and avoid shame if I am highly productive getting a lot done." Establish image of highly loyal, responsible, always there for the task, always gets the task done. Sacrifice whatever it takes to maintain this image. Guilt trip, accuse of ingratitude anyone who objects to the sacrifice. Portray boss as demanding, work as urgent, self as too kind to let co-workers down. Focus on the good of the cause, esp. God's work, or the crucial need for the income. Speak desperately of wanting to change lifestyle, negate any suggestions of how, deny emptiness regardless of success.

13. **Materialism:** "I only have worth and avoid shame if I gain a certain level of wealth, financial freedom, and / or very nice possessions." Establish image of quality-minded; become expert on details of material things; set goals of things to acquire—prioritize goals and stay focused; set new goals as needed; be vigilant to replace the out dated; protect and maintain things with whatever it takes *(covers, guilt tripping, rage)*; cope with jealousy by finding flaws in possessions of others, deny emptiness regardless of success.

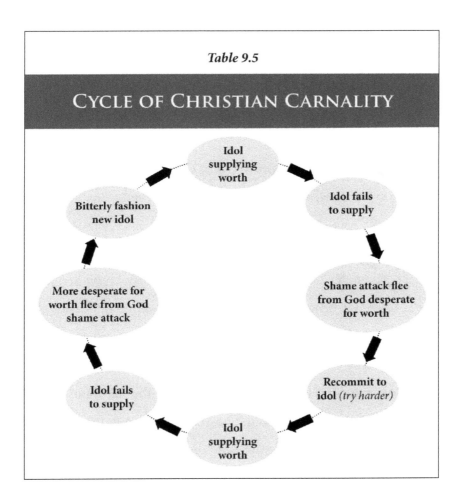

Table 9.5

CYCLE OF CHRISTIAN CARNALITY

Idol supplying worth

Idol fails to supply

Bitterly fashion new idol

Shame attack flee from God desperate for worth

More desperate for worth flee from God shame attack

Recommit to idol *(try harder)*

Idol fails to supply

Idol supplying worth

Chapter 10

Shame and Repentance

"And do not grieve the Holy Spirit of God, with whom you were
sealed for the day of Redemption."
Ephesians 4:30

stately, well groomed middle-aged woman arrived in my office. Her poise suggested self confidence. But tension in her body soon became apparent. As the story unfolded of her husband having disclosed an affair several months ago, it became obvious that their attempts to rebuild the marriage had not been totally successful. Although he was speaking words of regret, going with her to marital therapy, and obviously making an effort to be thoughtful and considerate, something was still wrong with their picture. She bravely explored the myriad feelings she had wrestled with since the disclosure. And then she seemed to land on the missing piece. Despite his consistent effort to be a model husband, the piece that kept her heart from mending was that he was not relating to her broken heart. When marital infidelity brings a couple to my office, often the betrayed one identifies a significant part of the pain as this: that while the betrayer acknowledges the moral wrong doing, there is a lack of being in touch with the broken heart of the betrayed one. It is an intimacy issue.

In a similar way, we may have an intimacy issue in our relationship with God. In order for our prayers to be a heart-to- heart communion with God, we must be well acquainted with His heart, as well as our own. Therefore understanding God's heart becomes key to building a relationship with him. Referring to Chapter 6, our own hearts must be well integrated and sufficiently known; the good, the bad, the ugly. Then when a significant understanding of God's heart and our own has been granted to us, we are ready to have real communion with God. But before we examine God's heart toward us, let's take a look at where our heart may be in relation to Him.

Table 10.1 can be used to assess our spiritual life. If we can understand where we are in our spiritual journey, we can decide if we want to be elsewhere. Or we are more likely to sense a nudge from the Holy Spirit calling us to move to a different place, be elsewhere, once we have identified where we are now. This simple assessment, at the risk of over simplifying, is designed in three letters to God. May each of us approach these letters, that represent spiritual stages, in openness and honesty. Ask God for discernment as you read these letters. They represent three possible stages of a spiritual journey. Turn to Table 10.1 and trust in the gift of discernment as you read.

And notice if anything in your life seems fitting for the blanks in any of the letters.

Now that you have read the letters, hopefully your heart is better known to you – especially regarding its relationship to idolatry. This understanding can inform your prayers about your spiritual growth.

As referenced above an important perspective in the healing process concerns God's heart. Norman Wright in <u>Always Daddy's Girl</u>[1] created an application of 1 Cor. 13: 4-8 to God's love for us that served as the inspiration for the following application of that same passage. Table 10.2 applies those verses to God's heart regarding us and shame. Turn to 10.2 and fill in the blanks with a form of the word shame. Let your heart be warmed and encouraged by these applications of His word.

After pondering these applications, we may ask ourselves: Do we deeply believe God has a covenanted shame-free heart in His relationship with us? A part of the healing process, in chapters 11 and 12, will refer to the description in Table 10.2 of God's shame-free heart. Our holy God never shames His sinful children. Thus we have one of the many reasons that any participation in shame on our part grieves God. This application of scripture in Table 10.2 creates a wonderful segue into a discussion of repentance. We need to know God's unchanging, loving heart for us at all times. But especially do we need to be mindful of His awesome love when we are convicted of having sinned and need to repent. We will be considering the difference in worldly sorrow and Godly sorrow.

"...For you became sorrowful as God intended...
Godly sorrow brings repentance that leads to salva-
tion..." 2 Corinthians 7:9-10.

In particular, we are looking at the role shame plays in the way we experience repentance.

In Hosea 7: 14, the prophet declares, "They do not cry out to me from their hearts but wail upon their beds." Another passage, Hosea 6:1-4, presents Israel as turning to the Lord, as full of faith. Yet when we read on to see God's response to their turning to Him, we realize something is wrong with this picture in God's perspective. What appears to be repentance is not accepted as such by God. They are seeking relief – relief from the pain of the consequences. Their focus on their pain is a shallow focus. It needs to deepen. Their focus needs to go to the condition of their hearts. Therefore their focus never reaches the underlying sin – the sin beneath the sin. In the kind of repentance Judas exhibited, he experienced intense remorse and made restitution by returning the money attained in the bribery.

"When Judas, who had betrayed him, saw that Jesus
was condemned, he was seized with remorse and
returned the thirty silver coins to the chief priests and
the elders. 'I have sinned... I have betrayed innocent
blood." Matthew 27:3-4

And yet, we know he did not experience the rest, the quietness, the trust, the strength described in Isaiah that comes from Godly repentance.

> *"So Judas threw the money into the temple and left. Then he went away and hanged himself."* *Matthew 27:5*

> *"In repentance and rest is your salvation, in quietness and trust is your strength, but you would have none of it." Isaiah 30:15*

So with these examples in scripture, let us focus more specifically on how Godly sorrow and worldly sorrow relate to shame, as outlined in Table 10.3. We continue to define shame as loss of worth including any pseudo-worth that we may have been experiencing by pursuing a source of worth apart from God. We have also looked at how shame is produced and maintained by rule-keeping and by rule-violating. The paradigm is living by rules that appease the idols we worship in exchange for pseudo-worth. Therefore, the mind that is focused on those appeasing rules responds to sin/guilt with a perspective of "I broke God's rules." See Table 10.3. While that may appear to be useful truth, it is shallow because it does not consider either God's heart or our own heart. And this is like the intimacy issue referred to in some marital betrayals at the beginning of this chapter. Likewise our relationship with God becomes more intimate when we begin to consider His heart more than we consider His rules.

Jesus brought a gospel that focuses on the condition of our hearts. He angered and exasperated the rule keepers. Some of his sternest rebukes were toward those Pharisees who focused on how their behavior demonstrated their ability to keep the rules, securing their righteousness and their worth.

> *"Woe to you, teachers of the law and Pharisees, you hypocrites! You clean the outside of the cup and dish, but inside they are full of greed and self-indulgence."*
> *Matthew 23:25*

Therefore let us use the revolutionary heart-focus brought by Jesus to turn our attention to God's heart. In that moment of conviction of sin, the shame-free repentant sinner is able to realize "I broke God's heart". Just as Jesus looking over Jerusalem wept for her lost condition, we can know God grieves when we sin.

> *"As he approached Jerusalem and saw the city, he wept over it..." Luke 19:41.*

When we remember God's grieving heart, we can stop focusing on our assumed loss of worth brought about by our sin. Likewise, we can relate to God's grief and be sad because of that consequence of our sin – His grief. Whereas those experiencing shame-based repentance may fear consequences such as lowered self-esteem, damaged reputation, and/or pride being hurt. They also may fear abandonment by God and/or others.

In contrast shame-free repentance produces sadness about our attitude, the condition of our heart- a condition that makes us vulnerable to sin in the first place. Those deep underlying conditions, the sin beneath the sin, may be a coldness toward God, unbelief in any of the attributes of God, failure to trust Him and/or denial of His goodness.

Ultimately the regret needs to be about sinning against God; about dethroning Jesus as our source of worth and thus grieving God. Instead, shame-based sinners focus regret on what they did or failed to do. Ultimately the shame-based sinners' regret is about the lack of ability to be perfect, to stay sin-free. Shame-free sinners are able to own their finiteness and take responsibility for their behavior and the idolatrous condition of their hearts. Whereas shame-based sinners shift the blame for the wrong-doing to others or to circumstances that provoked the behavior just as Adam and Eve did in the original sin and shame experience.

> *"The man said, 'The woman you put here with me-she gave me some fruit from the tree, and I ate it...The woman said, 'The serpent deceived me, and I ate'." Genesis 3:12-13*

If the shed blood of Jesus is our source of worth, then sin can be seen as the height of ingratitude for His shed blood, for all that was accomplished on Calvary that day. (Whereas shame blinds us to seeing any relationship of sin to ingratitude.) In that gratitude, freedom from shame allows us to be grateful beyond measure for His grace and His forgiveness. Otherwise we have a shame attack about being capable of sin and therefore, unworthy of forgiveness. Gratitude is not even on the radar screen. This shame then leads to a hatred of the behavior–so far so good. But, alas the hatred extends to the self. Whereas the shame-free are able to hate the sin – the behavior/the attitude/the idolatry – NOT the self.

Continuing with Table 10.3, we see that shame-free sinners desire to confess to God and the other if, as is usually the case, the sin has also been against another. The shame-based sinners' desire is to conceal. In the shame of having sinned, in this assumed loss of worth, the motivation is to hide, to take every measure necessary to create a secret about our sinful nature having reared its ugly head.

Under *Beliefs* in the left-hand column of Table 10.3 are truths from Calvary. In the opposite column are unbiblical beliefs that expose our carnality. (This pity party is compliments of our finiteness.) Again, we notice in this section the focus on what Christ accomplished on the cross, versus it is all about me. Shame-based sinners may paint self portraits of wretchedness, deceptively looking so humbly repentant. Actually these beliefs are shaming. So our shame gets reinforced and maintained by this mind-set. This self-focus crowds out the blessed awareness of God's grace and the resultant gratitude produced by recognizing His grace.

Under *Beliefs*, in the shame-free column we see the sufficiency of God's grace. Or in the right hand column, we see shame doing its dastardly deed by keeping the focus on self and the loss of pseudo-worth. And we will continue to see all the way down the shame-based repentance column, shame keeping the focus on self, on the big "I". Even a hatred of self exposes an exaltation of self- all of which is an unbiblical attitude.

The beliefs that prevail in Godly repentance have to do with the grace of our Lord. Believing that His grace is sufficient, we can know that He will never abandon us. He loves us as He loves Christ, even in the midst of convicting us of sin. We can be free of the fear of punishment because Jesus took the very wrath of God for us. We can stand firm that we are eternally His. What could I do that His amazing grace can not sufficiently bear?

The shame-based sinners continue a self focus about their hopelessness and worthlessness. Their failure thrusts them into a self perception of being a worthless failure because they cannot measure up as a keeper of the rules. Their experience of shame annihilates their experience of the grace of God. This is a vivid picture of shame-based carnal living.

So how do each of these scenarios end? What is the outcome of the shame-based approach that is self-focused with shame derailing Godly sorrow? And what is the outcome of the shame-free approach

where the sinful nature can be owned with a focus on God's cove-
nantal grace?

The last stage of Table 10.3 is the recommitment stage –
recommit to. As we might expect, the shame-based sinners continue
their "I" focus by recommitting to a trust in themselves. And so they
recommit to trying harder; to never doing this again; to going back to
being perfect. Their determination creates a drivenness to avoid sin
and to avoid any risk of shame-filled failure. Ultimately their recommitment is about regaining their pseudo-worth. The goal of perfection is reinstated. And the path toward these goals are strewn with
rule-abiding works. As we saw in the Cycle of Christian Carnality in
chapter 9, the shame-based sinners either recommit to the same old
idols or establish new ones. Either way they resume a very hard life
of carnality where they trust in their own determination and effort.
The recommitments in the right-hand column of Table 10.3, under
recommit to motivate us toward works. Again the focus is on "I".
And the expectations of performance constitute a do-it-yourself job
of securing our own worth. All of the planned and hoped for change
is empowered by self's determination and effort.

The left-hand column regarding recommitment is bathed in grace
and mercy. These commitments represent turning from our idol by
trusting, believing, walking, and relying on the power of the Spirit.
This way of living out our faith is depicted in Table 10.4 as the Cycle
of Christian Growth on the following page. This cycle is in direct
contrast to the Cycle of Christian Carnality, Table 9.4, in chapter 9.

Notice at the top left, the stage *Repent of idolatry*. This repentance refers to the shame-free column in Table 10.3 and the enjoyment of His amazing grace. Following the cycle down on the right side, the next stage is one of prosperity. But notice that we are most vulnerable for idolatry when we are prospering. Our finite nature is lulled by the prosperity – lulled into experiencing less need of God, less gratitude for His blessings. And some part of our success insidiously creeps up to the throne of our inner being and becomes so necessary for our worth that it is enthroned as an idol. Once again in His mercy, the idol fails to supply. But notice the crucial difference of responding to a shame attack in the cycle of Christian Growth. Instead of fleeing from God, we flee to God. And our repentance is one of depth and heart to heart. Thus we would all do well to be aware in our times of success of our vulnerability. Whatever the prosperity may look like, we want to be intentional about remaining grateful for the blessing. And in our gratitude, we can rejoice, enjoy our success, and even celebrate with lots of partying. But to lessen our vulnerability, we can stay mindful that NO success has any relationship to our worth, remembering that nothing we do or fail to do has anything to do with the value God places on us.

Actually this pattern of our faith at work in Table 10.4 is more accurately understood as a spiral. The growth experienced in this pattern finds us circling less frequently through the failure of an idol because we are increasingly trusting God as our source of worth and becoming less prone to idolatry. Also the time involved from a shame attack to Godly repentance becomes shorter as we grow. Additionally our repentance deepens. This is a picture of redemption and transformation, moving us from shame to glory.

> *"And we ... are being transformed into his likeness with every-increasing glory, which comes from the Lord, who is the Spirit." 2 Corinthians 3:18*

This last stage in Table 10.3 for the shame-free sinners is a reminder that the aspect of shame-free repentance is led and empowered by the Holy Spirit. Repentance for increasingly shame-free sinners finds the condition of their hearts more and more characterized by trust in God for worth, believing how valuable we are to Him. As we experience healing of our shame, we are more open to receiving God's forgiveness, giving thanks for it, and thereby glorifying our Lord. Our intimacy in our relationship with God deepens. We increasingly experience the power of the Spirit, as we yearn for the reality of the word of the Lord:

> *"... 'Not by might nor by power, but by my Spirit,' says the Lord Almighty." Zechariah 4:6*

And so practicing Godly sorrow where shame does not dominate our experience of repentance is an essential step into the process of being healed of our shame. The next chapter will explore the divine plan of transformation of our shame and the part we play in that transformation.

Table 10.1

LETTERS TO GOD FOR THREE STAGES

Stage 1: Communicating / Not Repenting

Lord, it's good to have you, but there's this other thing I need, _____, to really feel significant and worthwhile. Without it, I absolutely feel worthless. You are just not quite enough. In fact, if you take this thing from me, I will be bitter towards you. I would turn my back on you. You are negotiable, this is not. This is the real necessity of my life. If you are not useful to me in achieving it, I will turn on you. You know I grew up counting on this thing. I was so shamed, I had to get some worth from somewhere. It's not fair that I have to give it up. It's all the worth I've ever known. What will I have if I give this up? I have heard that I was designed to get my worth from you. But I'm just not ready to go there right now. Thanks anyway.

Yours in bondage, _____
(your name here)

Stage 2: Willing to be Made Willing

Lord, I am beginning to see how repulsive idolatry is—how my heart has taken this good thing, _____, and made it more important than Jesus. That I have given this thing the power to determine my worth. I have refused to get my worth from you. Now I see that the idol I fashioned hasn't remained under my control. It controls me. It requires service and obedience of me. I have lived in bondage to this because I thought I had to have it. Now my heart is softening toward Jesus as Lord, as my only source of worth. Please don't give up on me. Please continue the good work you have begun.

Hopeful in you, _____
(your name here)

Stage 3: From Shame to Glory

Lord, I am sick and worn out from controlling and being controlled by this idol, _____. I come to you repenting of having gone my own way to secure my worth. I regret grieving you by rejecting the worth you bestowed upon me. Yet you've loved me just the same. That kind of love is foreign to me. Your love, your forgiveness is beyond my understanding. Yet, by the power of your Spirit, I surrender into your grace and partake of it and rest in the reality that my worth is as secure in you as my salvation. I am grateful beyond measure.

Your beloved, _____
(your name here)

Table 10.2

BECAUSE GOD LOVES ME

(1 Corinthians 13:4-8 applied to shame: fill in blank with shame(s), shaming, shamed).

Because God loves me...

1. ...He is patient and kind with me, never _____ me.

2. ...He takes the seeming failures of my life and uses them in a constructive way for my growth, rather than _____ me about them.

3. ...He does not treat me as an object to be possessed and manipulated, which would _____ my personhood.

4. ...He has no need to impress me with how great and powerful He is because He is God. Nor does He belittle me as His child in order to show me how important He is, which would _____His respect of me.

5. ...He is for me. He wants to see me mature and develop in His love, refusing to _____ me by feeling hopeless about me.

6. ...He does not _____ me for making a mistake.

7. ...He does not keep score of all my sins and then beat me over the head with them, _____ me whenever He gets a chance.

8. ...He is not _____, when I do not walk in the ways that please Him. He is deeply grieved because He sees this as evidence that I don't trust Him and love Him.

9. ...He rejoices when I experience His power and strength and refuse to believe _____ messages for His name's sake.

10. ...He keeps working patiently with me even when I feel so _____ and think about giving up. He never _____ me by thinking about writing me off.

11. ...He keeps on trusting me, never _____ me, when at times I don't even trust myself and _____ myself.

12. ...He never _____ me by saying there is no hope for me; rather, He patiently works with me, loves me and disciplines me in such a way that it is hard for me to understand the depth of His concern for me.

13. ...He never forsakes me even though many of my friends might forsake me and _____ me.

Table 10.3

RESPONDING TO GUILT	
Shame-free Repentance	**Shame-based Repentance**
"I broke God's heart."	" I broke God's rules."
Focus: my attitude (grieves God)	Focus: my behavior (lowers my worth)
Sad about my attitude toward God: • a coldness / resistance / unbelief • failure to trust • denial of the goodness of God	Sad about or fear consequences: • hurt my self-esteem / reputation / pride • loss of worth / shame attack • God / others will abandon me / won't love me
Regret sinning against God / dethroning Jesus as my source of worth / grieving God	Regret what I did or failed to do / that I am not perfect
I alone am responsible for my behavior and my idolatry	Others / circumstances provoked my behavior
See sin as the height of ingratitude for His blood validating my worth	See sin as unrelated to gratitude
Grateful beyond measure for His grace / forgiveness	Shamed that I am capable of sin and unworthy of forgiveness / no gratitude
Hatred of the sin—the behavior / the attitude / the idolatry—not self	Hatred of behavior and self
Desire to confess to God / brother / sister	Desire to conceal
Beliefs: • His grace is sufficient • He will never abandon me • I am loved as He loves Christ • I am eternally His • He took the very wrath of God for me and stayed there for me—what could I do now that his love could not bear?	Beliefs: • I am hopeless / worthless • I am failure / a reject • I cannot measure up • I am shameful • This is beyond His grace
Recommit to: • Having no other gods before Him • Trusting God alone for worth • Believing He is good • Walking in the Spirit, forgiven, giving thanks in all things, being His glory • Reliance on His grace	Recommit to: • I must try harder • I must never do this again • I should be perfect • I must not sin • I will not risk shameful failure • I have to become more worthy
All in the Power of the Spirit	*By my determination and effort*

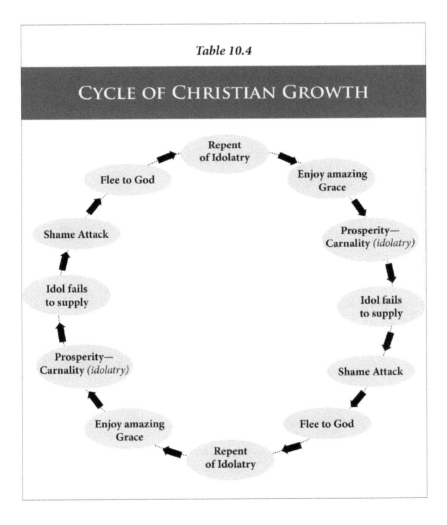

Table 10.4

CYCLE OF CHRISTIAN GROWTH

Repent of Idolatry

Enjoy amazing Grace

Prosperity— Carnality *(idolatry)*

Idol fails to supply

Shame Attack

Flee to God

Repent of Idolatry

Enjoy amazing Grace

Prosperity— Carnality *(idolatry)*

Idol fails to supply

Shame Attack

Flee to God

Chapter 11

Shame and Healing

"When Jesus saw him lying there and learned that he had been in this condition for a long time, he asked him, 'Do you want to get well?'" John 5: 6

As we turn our focus toward the healing of shame, let us recall the scene of Jesus healing the lame man in the above verse. We hear Jesus asking the crippled man if he wanted to be healed. At first glance that may seem to be a rhetorical question. However, Jesus may have had something quite powerful in mind as he queried the man. Whatever the extent of Jesus' purposes, it seems to have included having the man clarify and take responsibility for what he wanted. The crippled man is asked to participate in the healing process. In other scenes where Jesus heals, He calls for various kinds of participation. Sometimes the participation is more dramatic than simply verbalizing the desire for healing.

*"The man they call Jesus...told me to go to Siloam
and wash. So I went and washed, and then I could
see." John 9:11*

Thus we see that the one in need of healing, at a minimum, may be required to declare that he seeks healing.

I like to think of the seeker's participation as moving into or assuming a healing posture. The phrase healing posture is meant mostly in figurative terms, but not entirely. More about that later. The concept of a healing posture that is outlined in this chapter can be a way that our neediness and our faith in the Healer are expressed. God is the sole source of healing. Assuming this healing posture is how we focus our faith in the healing power that resides in God's will for us.

*"As the Scripture says, 'Anyone who trusts in him
will never be put to shame'." Romans 10:11*

One of the renown experts on shame deems it '...a sickness of the soul'[1]. Shame is truly a bondage. We are held captive to its diabolical control. Imagine how God desires to begin reducing shame's influence within our souls.

So what does a healing posture mean? The remainder of this book is focused on the healing posture, with guidelines for entering into that posture; guidelines for asking God to unwrap the layers of shame; guidelines for accessing that gracious gift of freedom from shame's deathly gripping bondage, guidelines for experiencing God's incredible mercy:

"He has sent me to bind up the brokenhearted, to proclaim freedom for the captives and release for the prisoners..."Isaiah 61:1

"There is, therefore now no condemnation for those who are in Christ Jesus..." Romans 8:1

We will consider the potential release from shame's control with three approaches. The alliterative categories are *Releasing, Refusing,* and *Reducing*. Remember to remain focused on the reality that God is the healer. These are recommended guidelines for declaring a desire to be freed from shame's bondage and assuming a posture whereby our faith is focused on the Healer.

The first category, *Releasing*, has to do with borrowed shame. The term borrowed comes from Table 4.7 in chapter 4. And there we can review examples of this type of shame. This is the shame that we inherit so well described by Ronald T. and Patricia Potter-Efron in *Letting Go of Shame*.

"Shame is contagious in shaming families. It can easily pass from one family member to another finally affecting everyone. This shame is transferred from its rightful owner to more vulnerable people. We call this shame "borrowed" to keep the focus on the possibility of returning it to its original owner. The idea is that at one time, a person was 'loaned' shame against his or her will. This shame originated from the behavior or attitudes of another, a usually more powerful family member. Now that shame must be returned before the healing person can embrace a non-shaming view of himself. All that is meant by returning borrowed shame is letting others take responsibility for their own behavior or feelings."[2]

This shame that is harbored in the family or the culture or the community is maintained by secrecy. If it is not an actual secret, simply having no freedom to discuss it also breeds shame. So notice in Table 11.1 that follows that the first guideline is to discover our story or borrowed shame. This discovery provides an opportunity to feel the grief and the anger about having this shame imposed upon us and others. If family members are willing to talk about the shameful issue, the secret, we have an opportunity to forgive those who participated in the shame, either by their actions or by maintaining the secrecy. Exposing the shame by discussing it is a step toward releasing it. Once borrowed shame is identified, our prayer can be one of asking God to grant us release from the shame and its consequences such as inferiority. Many of us find it helpful to use body language to express prayer, particularly for something like releasing shame. And so open, lifted hands could be helpful for this expression of faith. Truly God is glorified with our expressions of faith.

The next category in Table 11.2, *Refusing*, has two parts. The first part is about managing shame in the moment when we are being shamed. Please turn to part one now. Unfortunately, others are quite capable of sharing their shame with us, as we are with them. Also others can trigger our shame, though they may be innocent of a shameful attitude or shameful words in the moment. I had such an experience one day when my neighbor drove into his driveway in a new car. I walked across my lawn to join in his delight of his purchase. But his response to my compliment was downplaying and minimizing his purchase. Later he confided that he had some "bad feelings" because he had violated an ingrained family tradition when he purchased a new vehicle versus finding a good used one. His shame was stirred though I had only affirming, good will toward him. We do well to examine our words and attitude if the other person seems uncomfortable. But we can keep in mind that we may have only been a trigger for his or her discomfort.

When any of us are being shamed, we can know that the shame comes from other people's illegitimate attempt to manage their own shame. It is like temporarily getting rid of the shame within by passing it on to another person. Let us use a very simple illustration to see these guidelines in action. We have scheduled lunch with a friend and our arrival is delayed for a noteworthy amount of time. After hurriedly dashing in and sincerely apologizing, we are greeted with "I don't have all day you know", in a condescending, sarcastic tone that conveys "shame on you." First we need to realize that we are being shamed. Then remembering that the other is illegitimately managing his own shame helps to depersonalize its impact and buys us time – time to hold off the triggering of our shame. It is a way of setting emotional boundaries. If we are succeeding in buying some time and successfully refusing to internalize the shame coming our way, we can continue depersonalizing the shame by identifying the "shud" in the other's rule book that drives the other's shaming comment or body language. Though we usually cannot know the violated "shud" inside the other, we can imagine one. In this illustration, we can think maybe the other's rule book contains something like I "shud" always feel respected by others meeting me on time. Or we can just simply wonder about what is in his rule book that is triggered by my lateness. We know that this way of managing shame has a temporal effect because some people spend a lifetime of managing their shame by shaming others. When we are the recipient of the shame, we need to identify the shaming words or the shaming tone or a combination of words and tone that are shaming.

Continuing with refusing to internalize the shame, we need to avoid trying to prove them wrong. It is helpful to remember that this is about their management of their own shame. So trying to change their perspective is futile. For example, we might say something like, "Gosh I don't think I've ever been late before for our lunch dates." Introducing a different perspective does not move them out of their shaming moment because they are simply passing on their own triggered shame. Our behavior was merely a trigger for their shame.

This is not easy to do. We are so inclined to focus on the content versus the process. But once we recognize that the process is shaming, we will be better able to avoid trying to change the content. Another variation on this theme is to avoid trying to change ourselves in order to move our shamers out of their shaming mode. So that might sound like "I promise I'll never try a new route and risk being late again." Again that veiled plea for please stop shaming me will not work. Let me emphasize that I am only recommending we not make a direct plea to get someone to stop shaming us. But a response that conveys it is unacceptable that I be shamed is usually very appropriate. In fact, setting a boundary by conveying "I won't be spoken to in such a tone" and/or ending the conversation could be bolds act of love. This process of refusing shame may appear to be time-consuming and complicated. When first learning these guidelines, I recommend that we apply them retroactively. That is, after a shaming encounter, that we go back to those moments and see how the guidelines would apply. Thus we begin to memorize the ways to depersonalize the other's behavior, to leave the shame as being about them, and prevent our responding in kind by conveying "shame on you" for shaming me. As with any new behavior based on unfamiliar choices, the more the guidelines are practiced the easier to apply.

The second part of *Refusing* is about our initiating shame toward another. Please read part two now. The amount of shame stored in the dark crevices of our hearts corresponds to the likelihood of our shaming another. If we recognize we are at high risk for having our shame triggered and passing it on to another, healing of our shame becomes all the more an imperative. We start by identifying that we have shamed another. For an illustration see *Refusing*, Table 11.2, Part 2, imagining you are a relatively conservative parent of a 13-year- old daughter who steps out of her bedroom one day with enough makeup on to qualify her for show business. You didn't know she had acquired the makeup, much less that she would indulge in such contraband. Your reflexive horror reigns judgment on her, declaring that she not only looks like a slut, but she could win a contest of low-lifers. Hopefully we are shocked at our barrage of shame. And if we have started owning our finiteness, including our sinful nature, we will be able to acknowledge that our response was shaming. Remember that God's word declares the crux of our sinful nature.

> *"The heart is deceitful above all things and desper-*
> *ately wicked; who can know it?" Jeremiah 17: 9*
> *(The King James Version)*

We can know it. As we own our finiteness, we can release the desire "to be as God". Thus the Holy Spirit gains access to our souls. Then we can know the conviction sent by a loving and merciful God. In this illustration we can recognize having been a shamer. Then we can apply the guidelines given in Table 11.2, Part 2.

After practicing these guidelines and healing is underway, we will be able to head off our shaming impulse at the pass. We will begin to notice the shame arising within us and restrain its expression. However, in the beginning the best we can do may be to apply these guidelines retroactively. We may assume the healing posture by revisiting an encounter and discerning how the guidelines could have been applied. After being willing to own that we have shamed another, it will be helpful to remember that Romans 8:1 applies to the other person.

> *"Therefore, there is now no condemnation for those*
> *who are in Christ Jesus..." Romans 8:1*

This means that regardless of how the other has wounded us or disappointed us we are not to convey "shame on you." We may be understandably hurt, we may be legitimately angry. And we need to respect those feelings and manage them well. But what is never legitimate is for us to devalue another by shaming them. Shaming another is an automatic step up to superiority over the devalued other. It is not a step into the healing posture. Not only is it not a step into the healing posture, when we shame another person, we actually add to our own store of shame. The previous verses we have referenced make it clear that God never wants us participating in shame, either receiving it or giving it. The next step into the healing posture is to prayerfully identify the necessarily violated "shud" in our rule book by which our shame was triggered. We can then decide to delete it from our rule book or to renounce it.

In the illustration of the daughter laden with makeup, let us imagine that God reveals a "shud" in our rule book such as I must have children that express our family values. Or I must have children that never take a step into a wanton lifestyle. Or I must have children that always make Godly choices. Or I must have children that reflect my godliness. Then I will have worth and avoid shame. (Turn back to Table 9.4 in chapter 9 and reread no. 5 for other possibilities of idol appeasing "shuds" that God may reveal to us.) With the identification of the violated "shud" in our rule book, we are ready to identify the idolatry involved in the shaming of the other person. When God reveals the idol system involved in a given incident, His conviction calls us to repentance. We can accept the conviction of idolatry and repent. And in Godly sorrow we can reclaim our true worth from the only true source.

You will notice some overlap of guidelines for assuming a healing posture in these three categories of shame – releasing, refusing, and reducing. However, there are significant differences. So addressing the healing posture for each of the three types creates comprehensive guidelines for assuming a healing posture and seeking healing.

The last of the three categories is in Table 11.3, *Reducing, Part 1 and Part 2*. This focus is on the experience of having a shame attack. To review the experience of a shame attack refer to chapter 1. Again these guidelines are for assuming a healing posture. They help us flee to God as described in Table 10.4 in chapter 10. And they help us pray effectively for the healing we desire.

These guidelines in Table 11.3 are an acronym of *SHAME ATTACK*. Again these guidelines are to help us seek healing for the shame buried in our finite natures. Buried – but buried alive and wielding influence in a stealthy manner. The first of these guidelines is to recognize our own experience of having a shame attack. Please refer to each step as you read the commentary.

The "S" contains a concise definition of a shame attack as well as noting that even the first step begins to glorify God. Simply being willing to own that our stored shame has been triggered and has surfaced is facing a painful reality that starts to turn our shame into glory. Please refer to each step as you read the commentary.

The second step, "H", in Table 11.3 is about our belief in God's acceptance and recognizing our need for His wisdom. It may be useful to have something tangible to help us remember God's acceptance, especially when we experience ourselves so utterly despicable in the devastation of a shame attack. The tangible item may be something personal such as a particular Bible verse that conveys His never failing acceptance of us. Or we may use items from Table 10.2 in chapter 10. Remembering and trusting His acceptance of us, regardless of our own lack of acceptance, will become easier as healing progresses. As our faith grows we may find that we no longer need anything tangible to remember His acceptance of us. Remembering His unconditional acceptance and His wisdom and seeking that wisdom glorifies our Lord.

The next step, "A", has to do with being willing to experience the shame. The following principle may at first seem like trivial pop psychology. However it is a powerful and motivating truth. Perhaps you are familiar with it. "Jesus cannot heal what we will not feel."

This step is about sitting in the feeling. Our default choice is to escape this painful experience. We would rather bake a pie and take it to the neighbor, scrub the kitchen floor, bring flowers home to the wife, clean the garage, change the oil in the car, or mow the lawn. And, of course, these escapes of do-good busyness do not have near the destructive consequences of addictive escapes. Whatever escapes from the threatening shame we use, they are momentary. The shame we escaped (with some kind of compulsive, defensive, or acting- out behavior) waits in ambush to torture us in the aftermath of the escape. Shame is an established part of the cycle of substance abuse and getting sober again. And its part in the cycle of domestic violence has been identified for decades. Remember from Table 5.1 in chapter 5 that anything is better than feeling worthless. The escapes we create in attempts to avoid or numb the shame actually cause more suffering in the long run than the pain we sought to avoid in the first place. One author puts it this way, "The pain won't kill you... but running from it might." But being willing to feel the shame is not about sitting in this misery alone. This hellacious place of experiencing shame does not repel our God.

> *"If I ascend up into heaven, thou art there; if I make*
> *my bed in hell, behold, thou art there." Psalm 139:8*

We can blessedly sit in this misery with a totally accepting, all-wise God who is not shaming us. We are prone to do most anything other than experience shame. But as we resist escaping and invite

God to be with us, we can know that His grace is sufficient in this pain. And then we can know that as we invite Him into our experience of shame and practice His presence, He is glorified.

The "M" step of the acronym is about identifying the "shud" in our rule book that has been violated, exposing a disgusting, shame-laden part of us. For example, no. 4 in Table 9.4 in chapter 9 is a list of possible "shuds" for serving the idol of flawless character. As an example, let us imagine that a person caught up in this particular idol system realizes they greeted and exchanged pleasantries with a newly widowed parishioner, totally forgetting the person's recent loss. The requirements for appeasing this idol leave no room for any insensitive, rude, or self-absorbed moments, not even a momentary distraction that would make one appear insensitive, rude, or self-absorbed. So violating those "shuds" as in this example would plunge that person into the pit of shame.

After identifying the violated "shud", we move to "E". It is time to face our powerlessness. We need to recognize that we are powerless to always abide by the "shud". And our powerlessness includes the reality that the shaming experiences of childhood were not under our control. Also our powerlessness is evident in the reality that those shaming experiences in our past still wield influence over our behavior to this day. Our shame turns into His glory when we embrace our powerlessness. Note how Henri J.M. Nouwen addresses this issue:

"You have to say yes fully to your powerlessness in order to let God heal you. But your willingness to experience your powerlessness already includes the beginning of surrender to God's action in you. Your willingness to let go of your desire to control your life reveals a certain trust. The more you relinquish your stubborn need to maintain power, the more you will get in touch with the One who has the power to heal and guide you. And the more you get in touch with that divine power, the easier it will be to confess to yourself and to others your basic powerlessness..."[3]

Table 11.3, Part 2 is the second word of the acronym, beginning with "A". At this point we are guided into the center of the idol system depicted in Table 9.2 in chapter 9 to identify the idol. Continuing with the example of greeting the widow, we could be convicted of the flawless character idol (No. 4 in Table 9.3, chapter 9). When we can name the idol, the Holy Spirit is ministering conviction to us. And that is our merciful God's call to repentance. (For reviewing repentance, refer to Table 10.3 in chapter 10.)

The next step, "T", has to do with being open to receive God's forgiveness and countering any tendency to self-condemn with thoughts of thanksgiving. God is glorified when we repent as well as when we internalize His forgiveness and offer thanks.

The second "T" in Table 11.3, Part 2 is optional, but highly recommended. If we are blessed with a safe person in our life, then he or she can be a channel of God's grace to us, especially when we are responding to a shame attack. (To review a description of a safe person, refer to the comments in chapter 7, regarding principles no. 8 and 9 in Table 7.1.) To be concise, a safe person is one who rather consistently lives in God's grace. Considering shame as like a fungus that thrives in the dark of secrecy can motivate us to bring it into the light by sharing our experience. In addition to compassionately hearing about our shame attack, a safe person can encourage us to seek healing.

Next we need to recommit to the only true source of worth. The "A" is to acknowledge God's power to meet our needs, including worth. When we depend on the sufficiency of His grace, He is glorified. The verse given with this step may be very familiar to us. But it becomes wonderfully effective when we specify a need that we are trusting God to meet, such as being the giver and sustainer of our worth.

"And my God will supply every need of yours according to his riches in glory in Christ Jesus." Philippians 4:19

The fifth step, "C" in Table 11.3, Part 2 is circumstantially oriented. In our management of our shame, we may have sinned against another. To continue with the example of greeting a widow without remembering her loss, we might try to cover our lapse by saying something like, "I did not bring it up because the timing was not appropriate." So we would need to own that lie and confess to the other that we had lied to them. Confession followed by trusting God to cleanse us truly glorifies God.

And then the last step, "K", in these guidelines for seeking healing is designed to encourage diligence. We need to persevere in practicing these steps as often as we realize that we are participating in shame, either shaming another or being shamed or suffering a shame attack.

> "And let us not grow weary in well-doing, for in
> due season we shall reap, if we do not lose heart."
> Galatians 6: 9 (The Revised Standard Version)

The belief in God's desire to heal us and assuming the healing posture of these steps of faith profoundly glorifies our Lord. As we begin to experience our soul's freedom from the captivity of shame, we will rejoice in our inheritance of being finite but knowing God's transforming work within. When healing is underway, there will be situations or incidents that we will notice have not triggered a shame attack as in our past. Likewise we will notice that when others wrong us or disappoint us, we are not so inclined to shame them. In addition, our defensive, compulsive, or addictive behaviors which are an attempt to keep shame submerged will be less needed. Owning our finite nature as well as our sinful nature breeds compassion and empathy in our souls. Thus we become a safe person to be a channel of God's grace to others.

As we use these guidelines to seek healing, we will be able to sing of God's healing with the Psalmist:

> *"I waited patiently for the LORD; he turned to me and heard my cry. He lifted me out of the slimy pit, out of the mud and mire; he set my feet on a rock and gave me a firm place to stand. He put a new song in my mouth, a hymn of praise to our God. Many will see and fear and put their trust in the LORD." Psalm 40: 1-3*

May these guidelines inspire each of us to seek healing of our shame. And may the focus of our seeking be steadfastly fixed on the one true healer. The trust required in such a focus truly glorifies our heavenly Father.

The final chapter is a recognition of the need to maintain the healing that God so graciously bestows on His beloved child. The guidelines recommended for maintaining the healing are respectful, non-shaming ways we treat ourselves. God is just as grieved when we shame ourselves as when we shame another person. May we continue to be encouraged and inspired by the final chapter.

Table 11.1

RELEASING BORROWED SHAME
(ALSO KNOWN AS EXISTENTIAL SHAME)

Inherited because of Geography:

- The community you lived in
- The wrong side of the tracks
- Whether rural or urban

Inherited because of Family Characteristics:

- Poverty
- Level of education
- Types of employment
- Chronic illness
- Handicaps
- Mental illness
- Sexual scandal
- Abdication
- Domestic violence
- Religion
- Family size
- Appearance of home
- Condition of vehicles

The Healing Posture for Releasing Borrowed Shame:

- Discover your story.
- Grieve / be angry about the failures and the pain and the secrecy.
- Ask God to heal all involved.
- Forgive the ones who failed.
- Forgive the ones who carried shame about it with secrecy.
- Share the secrets, expose the shame, and ask God to take it from you.

Table 11.2

REFUSING SHAME

PART 1: WHEN BEING SHAMED—

- Refuse to internalize shame.
- Respect the instinct "something is wrong with this picture."
- If suspicious of being shamed, remember Romans 8:1 "...no condemnation for those in Christ Jesus." Therefore—no grounds for me to be shamed—It is ungodly that I be shamed for anything
- Do not attempt to prove the person wrong
- Pray for discernment—Is the other shaming me or has my shame been innocently triggered?
- Do not ignore your discomfort—Maybe respond with "This isn't working well for me, I'll get back to you later." Or I'm feeling ignored, minimized, mocked..."
- Identify the 'shud' (implied or explicitly stated) e.g. " You 'shud'...you need to... you had better...
- Identify shaming tones that are condescending, incredulous, disgusted, judgmental.
- Identify the part of you being shamed.
- Identify shaming words that assault character.
- Ask God for grace to confront the shamer without shaming in return.
- Plan to forgive.
- Plan to seek healing if experienced shame.

PART 2: RESISTING SHAMING THE OTHER—

- Respect the instinct "something is wrong with this picture" by noting own or other's defensiveness
- When tempted to shame, remember Romans 8:1 "...no condemnation for those in Christ Jesus." Therefore—no grounds for me to be shamed—It is ungodly that I be shamed for anything
- Identify your shaming thoughts / words / tones that are ignoring, minimizing, belittling, mocking
- Identify / disavow the "shud," implied or explicitly stated e.g. "You shud..." "You need to..." "You had better..."
- Identify the part of the other you see as shameful.
- If shame was expressed, ask forgiveness.
- Plan to seek healing for the shame you were managing by shaming another.

Table 11.3

REDUCING SHAME

PART 1: SHAME

See the "bad" feeling for what it is—a shame attack
Ashamed (*split-off*) part of you has been exposed, exposing you as worthless. Part can be an actual body part or behavior (*something we did or failed to do.*) My shame turns into His glory when I face painful reality. *"There is a way that seems right...but its end is...death." Proverbs 14:12*

Hold onto God's acceptance / pray for wisdom
Remember God's acceptance...Ask God for the wisdom to apply these principles in this acronym to seek healing. *"If any of you lacks wisdom, let him ask God..." James 1:5.* God is the healer; we go down to the river and wash, but He does the healing. My shame turns into His glory when I hold onto His acceptance and seek His wisdom and healing.

Allow yourself to feel the shame and God's presence.
"If I ascend to heaven, thou art there! If I make my bed in hell, behold, thou art there! Psalm 139:8. Do not escape this emotional hell with compulsive or defensive behaviors! Consider God's grace as sufficient in this pain. His healing is worth the pain. My shame turns into His glory when I invite Him into my shame.

Make note of the violated "shud" and the exposed / shamed part.
Obeying your "shuds" is attempting to earn worth. *"...a man is not justified by works of the law but through faith in Jesus Christ..." Galatians, 2:16.* Own the part being shamed. My shame turns into His glory when I own a shamed part of me. *"If we say we have no sin, we deceive ourselves, and the truth is not in us." 1 John 1:8*

Embrace the powerlessness / power.
Identify where or how you are powerless—the idol you could not control and your shaming experiences in childhood. My shame turns into His glory when I embrace my powerlessness. *"He giveth power to the faint; and to them that have no might he increaseth strength." Isaiah 40:29*

Table 11.3

REDUCING SHAME

PART 2: ATTACK

Ask God to reveal the idol involved in this shame attack.
Realize you worship a source of worth, creating bondage *(obsession/ compulsion / addiction)*, which results in shame. Repent of this idolatry. My shame turns into His glory when I repent. *"But those who trust in idols…will be…in utter shame."* Isaiah 42:17

Take in the forgiveness and refuse further condemnatory thoughts.
My shame turns into His glory when I take in His forgiveness with thanksgiving. *"Therefore there is now no commendation for those who are in Christ Jesus."* Romans 8:1

Tell a safe person. One who knows God's grace, unlikely to respond shamingly, and likely to *"Let no corrupt communication proceed out of (his or her) mouth, but that which is good to the use of edifying, that it may minister grace unto the hearers."* Ephesians 4:29. My shame turns into His glory when I trust Him to provide a safe person.

Acknowledge God's power to meet your needs, including worth.
Recommit to Him as the source of worth. My shame turns into His glory when I trust Him to meet my needs. *"And my God will supply every need of yours according to his riches in glory in Christ Jesus."* Philippians 4:19.

Confess any sin against God and / or others, and be cleansed.
Sin may include shaming judgment toward another who originally shamed you. *"If we confess our sins, he is faithful and just to forgive us our sins, and to cleanse us form all unrighteousness."* I John 1:9. *"…with the judgment you pronounce you will be judged…"* Matthew 7:2. My shame turns into His glory when I trust Him to cleanse me.

Keep doing all the above so God can begin freeing you.
God determined your worth. Other sources are idols. Be freed of this bondage of idolatry.

Chapter 12

Shame and Maintaining Healing

"Don't you know that you yourselves are
God's temple and that God's Spirit lives in you?"
1 Corinthians 3:16

ince you have stayed the course to this final chapter, con-gratulations are in order for you. Perseverance through all these aspects of shame commend you as a pilgrim willing to involve yourself in learning even when the material includes harsh realities. Your willingness to apply these harsh realities to your experience of life is admirable. Your healing is waiting in the wings where angels dwell.

As we begin to use the guidelines for seeking healing, know that something good this way comes for us. And most importantly know that God desires to transform our shame into His glory.

The onset of healing will manifest itself in varied ways. Some of us will step lightly into a long forgotten interest or undeveloped talent. Some of us will begin to enjoy a new found freedom from self-protection as the layers of shame are melted away in God's response to our request of Him. Openness and honesty about who we are will be easier for us. The defensive behaviors that protected us from shame attacks will become increasingly useless. (For a review of examples of defensive behaviors, see Chapter 5, Table 5.1.) Some of us will begin relating to shamers with a new-found assertive confidence. Some of us will sadly start recognizing our own tendency to shame others and will start deleting the "shuds" from our rule books that drive that habit so that it becomes an extinct habit. Some of us will begin to recognize a shame attack and see it as an opportunity to flee to our Lord for healing of the shame that is layered around a particular part of us. As the healing progresses we will realize an incident, that in our past would have triggered a shame attack, no longer produces that painful shame. Some of us will identify the blessing of a safe person in our life and have an increased desire to be a safe person for someone else. The list of possibilities is as lengthy as this book. Whatever direction the initial healing takes, it will be glorious. So our final focus concerns the maintaining of the healing as we become aware of His transforming blessings.

One theme in this last chapter concerns treating ourselves with honor so as to avoid shaming ourselves. This theme is about recognizing any dishonor that we extend to ourselves because any dishonoring behavior is shaming behavior. We have clearly seen that God grieves about any shaming we extend to others. The same holds true for treating ourselves shamefully. Whether it is toward another or toward ourselves, we are participating in shame. And that is never of the Lord or what He wants for us.

I also have come to believe that consistently treating ourselves with respect builds a kind of immunity against taking on new shame. Refusing to internalize shame becomes easier when we characteristically honor ourselves. The more we practice treating ourselves appropriately, as a beloved child of God, the less tolerant we will be when we are being shamed. And thus our tendency to internalize new shame will start to be reduced.

The dynamic of dishonoring one's self is frequently referred to as *beating up on myself*. Another reference used by those familiar with this material is *I've been shudding on myself*. These are references to the self-infliction of punitive shame by legalistically applying a law from our harsh rule book. This punitive legalistic use of "shud" does not facilitate repentance. In fact those self-condemning thoughts take position atop our slippery slope and have a high probability of plunging us down into the pit of shame. Even when we are convicted of having sinned, we can respond by repenting without any participation in shame. (To review the difference in worldly sorrow and Godly sorrow, refer to Chapter 10, Table 10.3.)

My favorite biblical example of shame-free conviction, is Nathan's confrontation with David in 2 Samuel 12. Nathan began by engaging David in a relevant story about an abundantly blessed man who robbed a man who had little. Then Nathan applied the principles of the story to David.

> *"Why did you despise the word of the Lord by doing what is evil in his eyes?" 2 Samuel 12:9*

I am persuaded that Nathan was chosen for this most significant mission because he would deliver the hard word to David without shaming him. A shaming tone or words or both could have distracted David from realizing that this message and messenger were sent by God. But his conviction led to shame-free repentance.

So in addition to repenting without plunging down the slippery slope into the pit of shame, let us look at other ways we can extend honor to ourselves – ways we can live in the truth that our worth is unalterably established by God.

> *"Do you not know that your body is a temple of the Holy Spirit, who is in you, whom you have received from God? You are not your own; you were bought at a price. Therefore honor God with your body." 1 Corinthians 6:19-20*

Table 12.1 addresses our responsibilities in the stewardship God gave us for self-care as a way of describing self-honoring behavior. Turn and read these recommended responsibilities in Table 12.1 now.

These responsibilities for self care can be summarized as examples of demonstrating maturity which is reflected in the following verse:

"When I was a child, I talked like a child, I thought like a child, I reasoned like a child. When I became a man, I put childish ways behind me." 1 Corinthians 13:11

More specifically, these responsibilities can help us to avoid the following:

- The internalizing of shaming judgments extended to us (note no. 1)
- The obligation to justify our choices and behaviors (note no. 2)
- Allowing another to determine our obligations (note no. 3)
- Requiring myself to know what I did not or do not know (note no. 7)
- Requiring others to read my mind (note no. 12)
- Over dis-closing (note no. 12)

In addition, these responsibilities leave us freedom for the following:

- To change my mind without justifying the change (note no. 4)
- To make restitution for mistakes without assuming a false guilt (note no. 5)
- To develop my own decision-making process (note no. 8)
- To ask for clarification without apology (note no. 9)
- To decide my own self improvement endeavors (note no. 10)
- To decide what is right for me (note no. 11)

- To make amends when I have been disrespectful (note no. 13)

The essence of these responsibilities is respecting and honoring the self, which God gave us stewardship over and thereby steering clear of shaming ourselves, His beloved. Remember the focus is about maintaining the healing of our shame and building an immunity against taking on new shame.

One author addressed honoring ourselves with a focus on our grooming habits and our conduct. The following recommendations in Table 12.2[1] are honoring habits that can also serve to remind us that our worth is unalterably established by God. Turn to Table 12.2 now and take your time as you read through it.

These suggestions are very straight forward. But notice that many of them call for significant change. If we realize that we have been shaming ourselves with behavior that is opposite of the suggestion, we need to be aware that the change will be a significant project. But if the Holy Spirit calls us to a significant change, He will provide the necessary wherewithal. For example, notice no. 1. If we drive a vehicle that would not pass a health department inspection, it will require much attention, energy and time to have our car consistently uncluttered, especially in the beginning. But as this honoring habit develops, every time we enter that car, the pleasure will provide an opportunity to remember that our worth is unalterably established by God. More about that later.

Other suggestions in Table 12.2 may stir emotions such as fear. An example could be Number 7. That recommended change may be difficult because we may fear the reaction of others when we say *no* instead of our usual *yes.*

You will note no. 10 is a reference to the "shudding" habit mentioned above as well as in Chapter 11, Table 11.3, Part 2, the first "T". A self- condemning habit is so blatantly a shaming habit. As mentioned earlier, we are to have no participation in shame, including shameful thoughts that are self directed.

Both number 11 and 12 are very positive ways to send ourselves a message reminding us about our unalterable God-given worth.

Increasing the ways we honor ourselves will have several benefits. It is true to a large extent that we teach others how to treat us. So when others observe us acting as people of worth, they are more likely to treat us likewise. Besides requiring courtesy and respect toward ourselves, simply treating ourselves in honoring ways influences others to treat themselves likewise. It is also true that our children and those under our influence learn about self care by watching us. So our habits of grooming and conduct convey to others whether or not we experience ourselves as people of worth.

While all of the above self-honoring recommendations in Tables 12.1 and 12.2 are valid, note this caveat. Employing any or all of the suggestions is totally unrelated to our actual worth. Please let us not leave this book with any doubts about our worth and the source of our worth. So when we increase the honorable ways we treat ourselves, our positive feelings about ourselves will increase. Let us be careful to recognize that these blessings are from the Giver of all good things. However these positive feelings are unrelated to our actual worth. Let these blessings stimulate gratitude for His mercy, love, and provision of our worth. So while our journey into the realm of shame will never reach completion, our journey in this material is ending. It has been vast, including many aspects of this stealthy emotion. It is so stealthy in fact that many of us are unaware of its presence, much less its influence and control.

Because this most painful experience can be buried, though buried alive, we have chosen hiding instead of healing. And in that choice we suffer distancing and alienation from others, as well as from God. Our journey began in the Garden of Eden. We could then see the question that continues to confront us. Will we remain in bondage to the shame-filled desire to be as God? Or will we rejoice in our inheritance as finite and beloved children of the Lord God Almighty?

Then our journey took us directly into the harsh realities of how we were shamed as children. And, of course, those harsh realities extend to how we shame others. And the destructive, vicious judgment "shame on you" spreads to include the next generation.

We looked at ways of managing our accumulation of shame with defensive behaviors that help keep our shame buried. We saw the results of shamed and split-off parts as a fragmented self that needs integrating. When those parts are owned, our integrity is strengthened. Then more of a self comes into awareness that we can then submit to the control of the Holy Spirit.

Another destructive result of shame was addressed as our unowned, undeveloped gifts, talents, and interests. The principles for experimenting or unleashing our creativity offer hope and encouragement to help us avoid going to our grave with most of our music still inside.

We then journeyed into the realm of differentiating shame and guilt in order to prevent guilt from taking us down the slippery slope into the pit of shame. The healthy management of any emotion or any need is the key to freeing it from any shame bound to the emotion.

Continuing to be brave readers, we confronted the reality of idolatry being at the heart of shame. Our idol systems maintain and promote the accumulation of shame. Thus we can know the mercy of God in the failure of our idol's provision of pseudo-worth.

Therefore understanding shame-free repentance was seen as crucial to our intimate relationship with God. Likewise we saw Godly sorrow (shame-free repentance) as vitally important to our empathically making amends with others.

The final focus was on assuming a healing posture related to the way we ask God for the healing He longs to bring to us. We examined releasing borrowed shame and refusing to participate in shame either by giving or receiving it.

Then we were encouraged to assume the healing posture when we recognize the experience of a shame attack. Each of the steps into a healing posture require us to trust in our Lord for His desire to bring freedom from the bondage of shame. God is glorified when His children pray for wisdom, remember His unconditional acceptance, humble themselves to be convicted of their idol system, and follow through with shame-free repentance. Each of the steps into the healing posture as we seek healing calls for a reliance on God as the healer.

Our journey approached its conclusion with recommendations for replacing self-shaming habits with habits of self respect. Living in a way that conveys our worth, unalterably deemed by God, brings Him glory.

Our final theme regarding the management and the healing of shame is on our relationship with God. And for that focus, let us return to the Garden of Eden. Remember the intimate relationship Adam and Eve enjoyed with God whereby they had an on-going infusion of worth. Originally they were content as finite beings in an intimate relationship with their infinite creator.

The gospel declares that the death and resurrection of Jesus restores our ability to have that intimate relationship with God. And in that intimacy he provides an on-going infusion of worth.

So the reality of intimacy with God stirs the question of how do we pursue and maintain intimacy with the God of the universe? Obviously the call of the gospel is to a repentant submission to the Lordship of Jesus Christ. What follows needs to be the development of a relationship of trust and obedience empowered by the Holy Spirit.

So as we see steps into a healing posture for God to lift our shame, there are steps we can take to deepen our relationship with Him whereby we can enjoy a continuous infusion of the worth he deemed for his beloved. There is a posture that invites and opens us to that constant infusion of worth. This posture would be like that described by the Psalmist:

> *"Blessed are those who have learned to acclaim you, who walk in the light of your presence, O Lord. They rejoice in your name all day long; they exult in your righteousness." Psalm 89:15-16*

The Christian community is blessed with myriad books about living out this relationship of faith. Various descriptions of activities that enhance our spiritual life can be helpful for creating a life line connection to God. One core element of those activities is taken from the example of Jesus' relationship with our heavenly Father during his earthly ministry. Scripture emphasizes Jesus' need for communication with the Father.

Three other themes are prominent in God's word. One is about our need for community, our need for fellowship with other believers. Another core element of this lifeline is about regular immersion in His holy word, both meditation and individual study, as well as pursuing anointed teaching and preaching. And a third theme woven throughout scripture is our need to worship the Lord of lords and the King of kings. Our worship, both privately and corporately is an essential and vital part of our lifeline.

So while these themes create disciplines to support our desire to trust and obey, there is a deeply personal dimension to this life-giving relationship. And that can be called practicing the presence of Jesus. This reference to our constant awareness of God includes trusting, obeying, giving thanks, and worshipping. For our reality is the belief that all good comes from our Father. And even our trials and difficulties are never without His presence. So an attitude of gratitude is always appropriate.

These themes of maintaining a lifeline connection to our Father whereby He meets our need to know our worth are not without danger. Remember that even Godly provisions can become idols in our vulnerable hearts. These disciplines can be legalistically practiced. When our attitude about any of the steps that deepen our intimacy with God crosses a fine line into treating the step as a law, we are then into works. The effort to enjoy God's grace can lead us into works. May we avoid this legalism by submitting to the leading and empowering of the Holy Spirit

> *"So I say, live by the Spirit, and you will not gratify the desires of the sinful nature... But if you are led by the Spirit, you are not under law." Galatians 5: 16-18*

May we know the work of the Spirit bringing inspiration and courage for seeking healing of this enemy of our souls. Praise be to our Lord for his sufficient and redemptive grace.

Our journey concludes with a letter to us from Jesus. This is a love letter that paraphrases the scriptures used in this book. Please fill in the blank in the opening with the name you are called by Jesus. And then open your heart to His heart to experience His love and His desire to heal and take us *From Shame to Glory*.

"My beloved _____ ,

Your attempt to be god-like,

    refusing to own your sinful nature

        or your finitude,

    has broken your heart,

        enslaved you in shame, and

            inhibited your giftedness.

May I heal you and set you free?

Then together we can face

    the sin,

        the uncertainty,

            the imperfection,

                and use your giftedness."

                            Love eternally,

                                Jesus

Table 12.1

AUTHENTIC RESPONSIBILITIES

PART 1

1. I alone am responsible for judging *(evaluating, assessing)* myself—my motives (intent, needs, feelings, spirituality, abilities, intelligence, priorities, values), and to determine any adjectives that describe me. Therefore, I may refuse any judgment of myself by others.

2. I am not obligated to answer to a human being for why I do what I do *(to justify my behaviors)*. That type of self-disclosure is a gift.

3. I have the responsibility to choose whether I offer help for other people's problems. I make my own commitments; no one can obligate me to that which I'm not committed.

4. I am responsible for taking care of myself, appropriately assisting those I'm committed to and seeking mutuality in friendships. I will sometimes change my mind. My new choice does not have to be justified and does not indicate that I have chosen irresponsibly.

5. As a human being, I will make mistakes. I am responsible to make appropriate restitution which may include expressions of regret or sorrow, but not guilt.

6. As a human being, I will sometimes not know the answer to a question. I am responsible to say "I don't know," and refuse any disrespect for "not knowing."

7. As a human being, I will sometimes act in a way that has unforeseen negative consequences for another. I am responsible for my own contribution to those consequences without requiring myself to have had prior knowledge I did not have.

Table 12.1

AUTHENTIC RESPONSIBILITIES

PART 2

8. As a human being, I will make some decisions that others may describe as illogical. I am responsible to make decisions according to all my senses, including my sense of logic.

9. When I do not understand any type of communication, I am responsible to ask for clarification without apology.

10. I am responsible for deciding if and what I want to improve about myself and responsible to refuse any disrespect for not wanting to improve in a particular way.

11. I am responsible to decide what is right for me, important to me, in my time frame.

12. I am responsible for appropriately self-disclosing—how I feel, what I think, and what I want, instead of withholding and requiring others to read my mind, or for telling them too much.

13. I am responsible for expressing myself without disrespecting another (*including being silent*); and, when I am disrespectful, to seek forgiveness, and plan to avoid repeating the disrespect.

I am responsible to require courtesy and respect toward me.

Table 12.2

TREATING YOURSELF WITH RESPECT

PART 1

1. Keep yourself, your surroundings, and your belongings clean.
   Personal application _____

2. Establish and maintain order in your life.
   Personal application _____

3. Behave in ways that are socially acceptable; mind your manners.
   Personal application _____

4. Dress up, and groom yourself to look your best.
   Personal application _____

5. Exercise, rest, and eat healthfully.
   Personal application _____

6. Protect your privacy.
   Personal application _____

7. Say no when you mean no.
   Personal application _____

8. Practice discretion in your relationships.
   You do not have to explain your whole life story to others. Choose how much of your life you want to reveal at any given moment, and give yourself permission to keep somethings to yourself.
   Personal application _____

9. Stop using foul language.
   Personal application _____

Table 12.2

TREATING YOURSELF WITH RESPECT

PART 2

10. Stop putting yourself down and making belittling comments about yourself.
 Personal application _____

11. Give yourself some time to enjoy each day and have some fun.
 Personal application _____

12. Bring beauty into your surroundings.
 Buy yourself some flowers, put a fresh coat of paint on your home, redecorate, listen to beautiful music etc.
 Personal application _____

13. Set new standards within the family for treating one another with respect. Explain to children what is respectful and disrespectful behavior, then require them to treat others with respect.
 Personal application _____

14. Do for yourself the things that are lacking related to a source of shame. For example, if you are ashamed because your parents never took you to a dentist and your teeth are a mess, make an appointment with a dentist.
 Personal application _____

15. Affirm yourself in the areas where you feel ashamed instead of waiting for someone else to fill this emotional void. For example, suppose somehow you experienced rejection of your masculine / feminine qualities, and you feel shame associated with your gender. Do things to affirm that part of yourself: buy clothes and accessories that help you feel masculine / feminine, treat yourself to a bubble bath, go to a typically male function, add something masculine / feminine to your life.
 Personal application _____

ENDNOTES

Preface

1. Pat Springle, *Overcoming Codependency*, (Rapha Publishing/Word, Inc., 1990), 161-2.

Chapter 1: Shame's Attack

1. Blaise Pascal, *The Fundamentals of the Christian Religion*, 1670, translated by W.F.Trotter, Douglas Editions, 2009, E-reader, unpaged.
2. John Bradshaw in seminar Washington D.C. 8/22/1992
3. Gershen Kaufman, *The Psychology of Shame: Theory and Treatment of Shame-Based Syndromes* (Michigan State University: Springer Publishing, 1992), 92
4. Charles Darwin *The Expressions of the Emotions in Man and Animals*, 1872,quoted by Donald L. Nathanson, *Shame and Pride*, New York: W.W.; Norton & Company, 141
5. Kaufman, 25
6. Ibid, 149-150

Chapter 2: Innate Shame

1. Margaret Alter, *Resurrection Psychology*, (Chicago, Illinois: Loyola University Press, 1994), 17

2. Ibid. 19-20.

3. Matthew Henry and Thomas Scott, *Commentary on the Holy Bible*, Nashville, Tennessee: Royal Publishers, Inc. 1979) 10.

4. Ibid. Alter, 17.

Chapter 3: Existential Shame

1. Theodor Seuss Geisel and Audrey S. Geisel, *Happy Birthday to You* (New York: Random House, Inc., 1987), unpaged.

2. Lee Ezell, *The Missing Piece* (New York: Bantam Books, 1987), 22, 31

3. "Lee Ezell's Story of Tragedy to Triumph", interview by Dan Wooding, accessed August 12, 2011, http://www. google.com/Lee Ezell/ About Lee.html.

4. Gershen Kaufman, *The Psychology of Shame: Theory and Treatment of Shame-Based Syndromes* (Michigan State University: Springer Publishing, 1992), 68.

5. C.G. Jung quoted by Julia Cameron, *The Artist's Way*, (NY: Putnam Publishing Group, 1992), 26.

6. Alice Miller, *The Drama of the Gifted Child*, (New York: Basic Books, 1997)

7. Carolyn Wells, Cheryl Glickauf-Hughes, Rebecca Jones, "Codependency: A Grass Roots Construct's Relationship to Shame-Proneness, Low Self-Esteem, and Childhood Parentification" *The American Journal of Family Therapy*, 27:63-71

Chapter 4: Personal Shame

1. Somerset Maugham, *Of Human Bondage*, (New York: Penguin Books, 1978) E-reader, unpaged

2. Charles Whitfield, *The Child Within* (Deerfield Beach, FL: Health Communications, Inc., 1987), 18 (compiled in part from Maslow, 1962, Miller, 1981, Well, 1973, Glasser, 1985)

3. Curt Thompson, *Anatomy of the Soul* (Wheaton, Il: Tyndale House Publishers, Inc., 2010) 11 – 26.

4. Gary Sibcy, "Emotion Coaching Your Kids", DVD lesson available at www.AACC.net/store, ECK-PTK

5. Ibid. Whitfield, 47

6. Tim Clinton and Gary Sibcy, *Attachments* (Brentwood, TN: Integrity Publishers, 2002), 15

7. Both Johnson and Greenberg have authored several books. Together they wrote *Emotionally Focused Therapy for Couples*, published by Guilford Press, 1988. John and Julie Gottman's writings include *10 Lessons to Transform Your Marriage* (Three Rivers Press, 2006)

8. Margaret Wilkinson and Alan Schore, *Coming Into Mind* (New York: Routledge 2006), 40

9. Clinton and Sibcy, 23-28, adapted from K. Bartholomew, "Avoidance of Intimacy: An Attachment Perspective," *Journal of Social and Personal Relationships 7* (1990): 147-178

10. Ibid. Clinton and Sibcy, 126

11. Ibid. 23

12. Ibid, Wilkinson and Schore, 40

13. Ibid. Clinton and Sibcy, 37

14. Ibid. Wilkinson and Schore, 39-40

15. Tim Clinton and Ron Hawkins, *The Popular Encyclopedia of Christian Counseling,* (Eugene, Oregon: Harvest House Publishers, 2011, 184

16. Ronald T. Potter-Efron and Patricia Potter-Efron, *Letting Go of Shame* (Center City, MN: Hazeldon, 1989), 154.

17. Morrison quoting Broucek quoting Tomkins, *The Underside of Shame* (Hillsdale, NJ: The Analytic Press, 1989), 53

Chapter 5: Defending Against Shame

1. Movie based on book, *The Secret Life of Bees,* Sue Monk Kidd, available DVD

2. Frank Minirth, Paul Meier, Stephen Arterburn, *The Complete Life Encyclopedia* (Nashville, Atlanta, London, Vancouver: Thomas Nelson Publisher, 1995), 540

3. Compiled from the work of Gershen Kaufman, *The Psychology of Shame*, (NY,NY: Springer Publishing Company, Inc., 1992)

4. Robert H. Albers and William M. Clements, *From Shame: A Faith Perspective* (10 Alice Street, Binghamton, NY: The Hayworth Pastoral Press, Inc., 1995), 72.

5. David Stoop, *Living With a Perfectionist* ((Nashville, TN: Oliver-Nelson Books, a Division of Thomas Nelson, Inc. Publishers, 1987), 59.

6. Thomas Moore, *Care of the Soul* (10 East 53rd St. New York, NY 10022, 1992), 148.

7. Lewis Smedes, *Shame and Grace* (NY,NY: HarperCollins Publishers), 92

Chapter 6: Integrity

1. Jill L. McNish, *Transforming Shame: A Pastoral Response* (10 Slice Street, Binghamton, NY: The Haworth Pastoral Press, 2004), 166

2. C.W. Neal, *Your 30-Day Journey to Freedom From Shame* (Nashville, TN: Oliver-Nelson Books, 1992), 69

3. Curtis A. Levang, *"The Adam and Eve Complex: Shame, Alienation, and Forgiveness"*: presented Christian Association of Psychological Studies conference: DVD available ITEC – 930424WKKC13

Chapter 7: Shame and Your Gifts

1. Erma Bombeck, quoted by Martha Williamson, online video @ beliefnet.com

2. Melodie Beattie, *The Language of Letting Go* (Hazelden Foundation,1990), 47

3. Joseph Chilton Pearce, quoted by Julia Cameron, The Artist's Way, (NY,NY: The Putnam Publishing Group, 1992), 29

4. Ibid. Cameron, 69

5. Ibid. Cameron, 33

6. Mark Twain, www.BrainyQuotes.com

7. Justice Oliver Wendell Holmes – www.BrainyQuotes.com

8. Peter Drucker, quoted by Julia Cameron, ibid., 207

9. Ibid. Cameron, 207

Chapter 8: Shame and Guilt

1. Joyce Meyer, www.BrainyQuotes.com

2. ibid, Albers and Clements

3. Gary A. Sibcy, Tim Clinton, and Ron Hawkins, "Interpersonal Neurobiology" Christiana Counseling Today, 20:14-20

4. compiled from the work of Andrew P. Morrison, *Shame: The Underside of Narcissism* (Hillsdale, NJ: The Analytic Press, 1989) and June Price Tangney, Ronda L. Dearing, *Shame and Guilt* (NY,NY: The Guilford Press, 2002), 25

Chapter 9: Shame and Idolatry

1. Matthew Henry and Thomas Scott, *Commentary on the Holy Bible*, (Nashville, Tenn: Royal Publishers, Inc., 1979), 10

2. Lynne Namka, *The Doormat Syndrome* (Deerfield Beach, FL: Health Communications, Inc.,1989), 62-64

3. Sarah Young, *Jesus Calling* (Nashville, Tennessee: Thomas Nelson, 2004), 90

4. John Witherspoon, quoted by Pastor Kokkola in "Character: What does it mean to be God Fearing and How do we get there and Why?", January 16, 2012, WordPress.com

Chapter 10 Shame and Repentance

1. Norman Wright, *Always Daddy's Girl* (Ventura, CA 93006: Regal Books, A division of GL Publications), 202-203

Chapter 11: Shame and Healing

1. Gershen Kaufman, *The Psychology of Shame: Theory and Treatment of Shame Based Syndromes,* (Michigan State Univ. Springer Publishing, 1992), 2

2. Ibid, Potter-Effron

3. H.J.M. Nouwen, *In Joyful Hope*, (Doubleday 1540 Broadway, New York, New York 10036, 1975), 99

Chapter 12: Shame and Maintaining Healing

1. Adapted from C.W. Neal, Your *30-Day Journey to Freedom From Shame* (Thomas Nelson Publishers, Nashville, TN), 112-114

Epilogue

*B*ravo for you who stayed the course through this book and are inspired to seek freedom from this diabolical enemy of your soul. May you be encouraged to stay on this pathway with the following summary regarding the process of being set free.

The healing posture is how we flee to God, hear from God, place our trust in Him, and begin to experience His release from the bondage of shame into freedom. This epilogue is a quick reference for you to use to assume the healing posture. Perhaps you will want to photocopy this page and the Tables from Chapter 11, "Shame and Healing," and Table 7.1 from Chapter 7, "Developing Your Gifts," and have these pages in a convenient location.

Foundational to the healing posture is faith the size of a mustard seed. After suffering a shame attack, you need only enough faith to choose to sit with God and employ these guidelines. This means exercising enough faith to choose to flee to God, in spite of the automatic assumption that He sees you as worthless. The first step is to choose which category of shame, as outlined in the tables in Chapter 11, applies to your situation. If the shame you have experienced has been active in the family, you would focus on the first category, borrowed shame, and follow those corresponding guidelines in Table 11.1.

If the shame comes from you being shamed or you shaming another person in the moment, you will need to focus on refusing, the second category. Following the guidelines in Table 11.2, Part 1 or Part 2 is assuming the healing posture for managing shame as it is happening in the moment.

The third category, reducing shame, regards anytime you recognize that you are having or have had a shame attack. Or you may notice that you have acted in a way that could be defending against or avoiding a shame attack. Or you may have noticed some thoughts about a creative endeavor that shame annihilates and takes you to "no way, not an option." Let this dastardly deed that squelches your creativity send you back to review Chapter 7, "Developing Your Gifts."

Applying the acronym in Table 11.3, parts 1 and 2 also ushers you into the healing posture. In this healing posture, God can reveal to you the details pertaining to your shame attack—details such as the "shud" in your rule book that was violated and the idolatry involved in your shame attack. The steps into the healing posture do not have to be taken in the order given. However, applying each step makes a complete statement of your desire for freedom and your trust in God to free your captivated soul. Let the last step in Table 11.3, part 2 encourage you to keep returning to the healing posture as often as you realize your reluctance to explore a creative endeavor or you recognize defensive behavior or you even suspect that you have had a shame attack.

Bless you, brave reader, as you continue your courageous journey on your pathway to freedom.

Remember:

"Being confident of this, that he who began a good work in you will carry it on to completion until the day of Christ Jesus."

Philippians 1:6

CPSIA information can be obtained
at www.ICGtesting.com
Printed in the USA
BVHW07s2013111018
529783BV00029B/725/P